T0248244

GREMLINS™

THE OFFICIAL COOKBOOK

16oz
1 CUP
8oz
1 CUP

GREMLINS™

THE OFFICIAL COOKBOOK

Recipes by Jenn Fujikawa

Written by Erik Burnham

INSIGHT EDITIONS

SAN RAFAEL • LOS ANGELES • LONDON

– *Billy*

CONTENTS

INTRODUCTION

Dear Billy,

Your father and I knew that one day your art would take you somewhere, but we never dreamed it would be all the way to New York! We are so proud of you–and Kate!–for everything you have accomplished since that Christmas with those nasty little creatures. (At least you know that nothing in the big city will ever be as hard to deal with as they were. I would call that a blessing in disguise, but I am not ready to go that far!)

I could not let you leave without something special to remember us by—after all, it is a Peltzer family tradition to send your children off with a gift that will either remind them of their old home or help them as they make a new one. And this cookbook can do both!

But it is more than that. A cookbook is like family history. Many of the recipes in these pages are dishes I have made for you a hundred times—like my famous Healing Chicken Soup (page 46) or the Homemade Fruit Leather you absolutely inhaled when you were in school (page 14). These foods can be a time machine, and it is my dear hope that you and Kate will add your own memories and recipes to this book and pass it on to your own children one day. (And there had better be grandchildren in my future, young man!)

Finding the right recipes and cooking them up helps me find a lot of joy. In fact, it is that joy that helped me get over the Christmas incident. I learned that making a dish that resembles a gremlin—and then eating it—is quite therapeutic. After all, it is harder to be afraid of something when its face is on a scone you are having with tea (page 74). But cooking is good for the little stresses, too, and I bet you can use this mindset to help you get through whatever New York throws at you. (I encourage you to do so! I want this book to be well worn and twice as thick when I get out to visit.)

I do hope this book will help you and Kate in your new life together. Sometimes a good meal (like your father's Five-Egg Omelet, page 52) is all you need to make the day easier to bear.

At the end of the day, whenever you use this book, whether to whip up one of my recipes or to add one of your own, I want you to remember how much we love you.

(And be careful on the subway!) –Lynn

P.S.: I HELPED YOUR MOTHER CATEGORIZE EVERYTHING, AND WE MADE SURE TO PICK THINGS THAT YOU CAN MAKE EVEN WITHOUT ONE OF MY INNOVATIVE, HANDY-DANDY INVENTIONS FOR THE MODERN KITCHEN. NOW, NO MATTER WHAT YOUR MOTHER SAYS, I WANT YOU TO KNOW THAT IT WAS ACTUALLY MY IDEA TO LEAVE A LITTLE EXTRA SPACE FOR YOU AND KATE TO ADD A FEW RECIPES OF YOUR OWN-SO TRY IT! IT'S FUN. (I'LL EVEN SHIP YOU MY PROTOTYPE TYPEMASTER 5000; IT'S LIKE A NORMAL TYPEWRITER, BUT YOU CAN PUT THIS WHOLE COOKBOOK IN IT TO MAKE SURE YOUR RECIPES ARE AS EASY TO READ AS ANYTHING PUBLISHED TODAY! IT EVEN TAKES DICTATION!) ENJOY THE BOOK, BUT REMEMBER: IF YOU EVER SEE GIZMO AGAIN, BE EXTRA CAREFUL WITH THE MIDNIGHT SNACK CAKES (PAGE 80). -RAND

Well, ah, future generations, I bet you're wondering why this cookbook looks like it went through hell. The answer to that is, because it did. I had the book with me in the art department at the Clamp Centre (I was going to use some office equipment to add some fun flourishes—don't judge me), and then somehow, the whole place was infested with gremlins. It made the Kingston Falls incident look like a walk in the park.

Anyway, the gremlins tore through every part of the building—including my cubicle. This book suffered some through the rampage, but it survived—just like a Peltzer. (I'm just lucky that the green menaces didn't set this book on fire. I never would've lived that down.)

But the experience got me thinking that most people don't have even one gremlin experience in their lives, let alone two. And since Gizmo is a part of our family, who knows if that will even be the last time? Maybe the gremlins are a curse we'll have to keep dealing with, an evil only our family can face, to keep humanity safe. Like my dad always said, nobody's got a story like this one. Nobody.

Any way you look at it, this book is a memento of all we've gone through and a reminder of our history. It's something I'll be proud to hand down, scars and all.

Kate and I have kept up Mom's wishes and added to the cookbook—and with luck, you will, too. It really is therapeutic! But never forget, whatever you do and whatever you make, don't give it to a mogwai after midnight! —*Billy*

Snacks

I admit, son, I got so invested in this little project that I decided to go all out and really make this cookbook the best it could be. That's when I realized, when you pick up a cookbook—even a homemade one—what you're really picking up is an instruction manual. That's why categorization is key! Say you're in the mood for something after a long day. You grab your cookbook off the shelf for some ideas, and you can find what you're in the mood for fast because, why? Organization. It's efficient! That's why this book you're holding in your hands is separated into five handy-dandy categories that run the full gamut of culinary possibility.

First things first: We lead off with snacks, a catchall category that can set you straight whether you're in the mood for something sweet, like Mr. Hanson's Candy Bar Salad (page 16), or something savory, like a bowl of Chinatown Wonton Soup (page 18). No matter what your palate is pushing for, you'll find something to satisfy it in the next few pages. (Just don't go spoiling your appetite before a big meal!) - RAND

GREMLIN FINGERS (GF, V, V+)

I read somewhere that pretending to destroy and eat something you are afraid of is therapeutic—and because of that, a few of the recipes in this book are a little bit . . . gremlin-y. We have had fried edamame pods before: They are a tasty snack and a nice side dish, but if you ask me, they also look like little gremlin fingers, so that is what I've decided to call them! And do you know what else? I do feel better after I eat them! That is proof that it works, as far as I am concerned. It is also why there are a few other gremlin-style recipes in this little project—but this one is the first, and it is my favorite. —Lynn

PREP TIME: 10 minutes
COOK TIME: 8 minutes
YIELD: 4 servings
DIFFICULTY: Easy

INGREDIENTS

16 ounces frozen precooked edamame
1 tablespoon olive oil
2 garlic cloves, minced
1 teaspoon chili flakes
1 teaspoon tamari
½ teaspoon sesame oil
½ teaspoon kosher salt

DIRECTIONS

1. Bring a large pot of water to a boil. Add the edamame, and cook for 2 to 3 minutes until heated through. Drain.
2. In a large skillet over medium heat, add the olive oil, garlic, and chili flakes. Cook for 2 to 3 minutes until fragrant.
3. Add the edamame, tamari, and sesame oil, and cook for 2 minutes until coated.
4. Transfer the edamame to a large serving bowl. Let cool for 2 minutes, sprinkle with salt, and serve immediately.

GREMLIN WINGS (GF)

You might be thinking that these chicken wings do not seem as gremlin-y as some of the other cheeky, gremlin-inspired recipes that I included in this book, but just wait. All they need is a little bit of salsa verde—which is just the right shade of green—and you will find that these wings are as gremlin-y as anything! (I know some people prefer ranch dressing with their wings, but I think this salsa is much better.) –Lynn

PREP TIME: 10 minutes
COOK TIME: 1 hour 5 minutes
YIELD: 6 servings
DIFFICULTY: Moderate

INGREDIENTS

Salsa Verde

6 small tomatillos, husked, washed, and dried
½ small white onion
1 small jalapeño, seeded
1 garlic clove
½ cup fresh cilantro, stemmed
½ teaspoon kosher salt

Chicken

2 pounds chicken wings
2 tablespoons baking powder
1 teaspoon garlic powder
1 teaspoon onion powder
1 teaspoon dried rosemary
½ teaspoon kosher salt
½ teaspoon black pepper
Fresh cilantro, for garnish

DIRECTIONS

1. Preheat the oven to 400°F.
2. To make the salsa verde: Place the tomatillos, onion, jalapeño, and garlic on a foil-lined baking sheet.
3. Bake for 20 minutes until the vegetables are softened and fragrant. Let cool slightly.
4. Add the roasted vegetables to a blender, along with the cilantro and salt. Blend until combined. Set aside.
5. To make the chicken: With the oven still set to 400°F, prep a baking sheet with a wire rack greased with nonstick cooking spray.
6. In a large bowl, toss the chicken wings with the baking powder, garlic powder, onion powder, rosemary, salt, and pepper. Place the wings onto the prepped baking sheet, and bake for 45 minutes until cooked through.
7. Pour the salsa verde over the chicken wings. Sprinkle with cilantro, and serve.

HOMEMADE FRUIT LEATHER (GF, V)

You might not remember this, Billy, but when you were a little boy, you loved that rolled fruit leather down at the grocery store. Whenever they ran out, you would have such an absolute fit that I knew I had to learn how to make it from scratch if I ever wanted any peace again! And after I did, goodness—I couldn't make it fast enough! I'm telling you now, when you have children of your own, you will want to know how to make this . . . especially if *your* son refuses to go to bed until he's had a snack! –Lynn

PREP TIME: 5 minutes (plus 2 hours for cooling)
COOK TIME: 4 hours
YIELD: 8 servings
DIFFICULTY: Easy

INGREDIENTS

2 cups strawberries, hulled and halved
2 cups raspberries
3 tablespoons honey
1 tablespoon lemon juice

DIRECTIONS

1. Preheat the oven to 150°F. Prep a baking sheet with parchment paper. Set aside.
2. In a blender, add the strawberries, raspberries, honey, and lemon juice. Blend until smooth.
3. Spread onto the prepped baking sheet to ¼ inch thick.
4. Bake for 4 hours. Remove from the oven, and let cool for 2 hours, or until cooled completely.
5. Use a pizza cutter to cut the fruit leather into 1-inch-wide strips. Roll up to serve.

I'VE BEEN WORKING ON AN INVENTION FOR THIS-THE PELTZER PRESS. MAKES FRUIT LEATHER AND IRONS YOUR PANTS AT THE SAME TIME! LET YOUR BOSSES KNOW I CAN HAVE A PROTOTYPE FOR THEM WHENEVER THEY'RE READY-KIDS'LL LOVE IT! - RAND

MICROWAVE POPCORN (GF, V)

Everything is more expensive in New York, sweetheart, so I want to remind you that popcorn is one of the best snacks you can have—and homemade popcorn is easier on the budget than store-bought bags and is also environmentally friendly! I have been making a lot of things like this since your father surprised me with a new microwave oven—we just could not get the smell of that gremlin out of our other one. I do not want to spoil your appetite, so I will not go into detail . . . except to say, there are some smells even bleach can't remove! —Lynn

PREP TIME: 5 minutes
COOK TIME: 3 minutes
YIELD: 4 servings
DIFFICULTY: Easy

DO YOU FIND YOURSELF GETTING BORED WITH JUST SALT AND BUTTER ON YOUR POPCORN? OF COURSE YOU DO. WHO DOESN'T? WHAT YOU GOTTA DO IS SPICE THINGS UP WITH A SEASONING BLEND. YOUR MOTHER'S FAVORITE IS CAJUN. YOU GOTTA TRY IT-IT'LL REVOLUTIONIZE THE WAY YOU SNACK. - RAND

INGREDIENTS

Spice Mixture

1 teaspoon garlic powder
1 teaspoon smoked paprika
½ teaspoon onion powder
½ teaspoon dried oregano
½ teaspoon dried thyme
½ teaspoon granulated sugar
¼ teaspoon cayenne pepper

Popcorn

¼ cup popcorn kernels
1 brown paper bag
1 tablespoon unsalted butter
½ teaspoon kosher salt

DIRECTIONS

1. To make the spice mixture: In a small bowl, stir together the garlic powder, paprika, onion powder, oregano, thyme, sugar, and cayenne pepper.
2. To make the popcorn: Add the popcorn kernels to the brown paper bag, and add the spice mixture and butter. Roll down the top of the bag to close it.
3. Place the bag in the microwave, and cook on high for 2½ to 3 minutes.
4. Pour the popcorn into a bowl, and sprinkle with salt.

MR. HANSON'S CANDY BAR SALAD (V)

I found this recipe in an old school newspaper of yours that I had saved—the Halloween issue, where your science teacher, Mr. Hanson, insisted there was no scientific evidence that a salad needed to include lettuce and "proved it" by sharing a recipe for an apple salad mixed with chopped-up candy bars. If anything was ever appropriate for a children's Halloween party, this would be it—so maybe you should keep this one in your back pocket for when you have kids of your own. (I promise I won't mention my future grandchildren on every page of this book!) —Lynn

PREP TIME: 15 minutes
COOK TIME: N/A
YIELD: 10 servings
DIFFICULTY: Easy

INGREDIENTS

5 large Granny Smith apples, cored and chopped (reserve 1 cup for garnish)
2 tablespoons lemon juice
1 cup whole milk
One 3.4-ounce box instant vanilla pudding
8 ounces frozen whipped topping, thawed
½ teaspoon vanilla extract
¼ teaspoon kosher salt
Six 1.86-ounce peanut nougat chocolate candy bars, diced (reserve 1 cup for garnish)

DIRECTIONS

1. In a medium bowl, toss the chopped apples with the lemon juice. Set aside.
2. In a large bowl, whisk the milk and pudding for 2 minutes until slightly thickened. Fold in the whipped topping, vanilla, and salt.
3. Pat the apples dry, and reserve 1 cup for garnish. Fold the remaining apples and all but 1 cup of the chopped candy bars into the pudding mixture.
4. Top with the remaining 1 cup of apples and the reserved 1 cup of candy bars, and then serve.

CHINATOWN WONTON SOUP

One of the great pleasures of life is learning to expand your palate and enjoy the food of other cultures. Of course, maybe you wonder why that's so—you're raised on what you like, you're comfortable with it. I get that—perfectly respectable position. But let me ask you this: What is it that people want most? To solve problems. Every job has one, and every problem has a creative solution. The secret to finding solutions is keeping an open mind. And that starts with food. That attitude has led me to discover how much I love a good wonton soup, which is right up there with your mother's Healing Chicken Soup for me (page 46). Even though you're within arm's reach of Chinatown, this is the soup you've got to try. (I gave a Bathroom Buddy to Mr. Wing's grandson in exchange for a couple of his mama's recipes. Let me tell you, it was one of the best deals I've ever made!) – RAND

PREP TIME: 45 minutes
COOK TIME: 10 minutes
YIELD: 8 servings
DIFFICULTY: Moderate

INGREDIENTS

Wontons

8 ounces ground pork
1 small shallot, diced
2 garlic cloves, minced
2 tablespoons oyster sauce
1 tablespoon soy sauce
1 teaspoon fresh ginger, minced
½ teaspoon sesame oil
¼ teaspoon white pepper
40 wonton wrappers

Soup

10 cups chicken broth
2 tablespoons soy sauce
1-inch slice fresh ginger
2 garlic cloves, finely minced
1 teaspoon sesame oil
½ teaspoon white pepper
2 green onions, minced, for garnish

DIRECTIONS

1. To make the wontons: In a medium bowl, mix together the ground pork, shallot, garlic, oyster sauce, soy sauce, ginger, sesame oil, and white pepper until just combined.
2. Place a tablespoon of filling into the center of a wonton wrapper. Use your finger to add water onto two sides; then fold them up and create a triangle shape. Pinch and fold the pointed corners downward. Dab water on the ends, then tuck them in. Place onto a parchment-lined plate, and cover with a towel. Repeat with the rest of the filling and wrappers.
3. To make the soup: In a large stockpot, add the chicken broth, soy sauce, ginger, garlic, sesame oil, and white pepper. Bring to a boil.
4. Add the wontons. Gently stir, to prevent them from sticking. Cook for 2 minutes until the wontons are cooked through and float to the surface. Discard the ginger.
5. Ladle into soup bowls, sprinkle with green onions, and serve.

DAFFY'S CORN ON THE COB (GF, V)

I'd never seen a mogwai eat before I was asked to bring Gizmo home from the Clamp Centre—what a pretentious way to spell *center*, right? And sure, it wasn't really Gizmo that I brought home, but that wasn't my fault. Mogwais all look so much alike! Anyway, I'd never seen a mogwai eat anything, and I wasn't ready for just how fast he powered through the corn on the cob that I'd given him. It actually reminded me of this nature documentary about predators I'd seen. I was eight or nine, and I was at school. It was science class, and I usually loved it . . . until . . . well—I think about it still. And now I also see that daffy little mogwai's face in my mind every time I eat corn. And when the corn has toppings, like this? With cotija cheese and chili powder? Well, then, I think I could eat even faster than he did! —Kate

PREP TIME: 10 minutes
COOK TIME: 40 minutes
YIELD: 4 servings
DIFFICULTY: Easy

INGREDIENTS

4 ears corn, in husks
4 wooden sticks
¼ cup mayonnaise
¼ cup crema
½ cup cotija cheese, crumbled
2 tablespoons chili powder
2 teaspoons smoked paprika
Zest of 1 lime
½ teaspoon kosher salt
Hot sauce, for serving
2 tablespoons minced cilantro
4 lime wedges, for serving

DIRECTIONS

1. Preheat the oven to 375°F. Place the corn directly onto the oven rack. Cook for 40 minutes; then remove from the oven and let cool slightly for 2 to 3 minutes. Remove the husks, and insert a wooden stick into one end of each ear of corn.
2. In a small bowl, stir together the mayonnaise and crema. Brush onto the corn.
3. Sprinkle the corn with cotija cheese, chili powder, paprika, lime zest, and salt. Then drizzle with hot sauce, sprinkle with cilantro, and serve with lime wedges.

JELLIED GREMLIN GUTS (GF, V)

My mom always made this gooey gelatin salad for Memorial Day cookouts. I used to love the cookouts we had on that holiday. I looked forward to them every year . . . until the incident . . . but never mind that. I don't want to put those details down for posterity—it'd ruin appetites forever. Let's just say that I never saw anything that gross again, including the mass of gremlin guts I waded through after an elevator at the Clamp Centre squished a bunch of the little creeps. And now all I can think of is how much this salad reminds me of the gremlin guts. Is it weird that that's comforting? After all, gremlin guts mean a dead gremlin, and a dead gremlin means safety. —Kate

PREP TIME: 30 minutes (plus 6½ hours of refrigeration)
COOK TIME: 10 minutes
YIELD: 6 servings
DIFFICULTY: Moderate

INGREDIENTS

Two 3-ounce packages lime gelatin
2 cups boiling water, divided
1 cup cold water
One 20-ounce can crushed pineapple, drained
1 cup vanilla Greek yogurt

DIRECTIONS

1. In a large bowl, whisk together one package of lime gelatin and 1 cup boiling water until the gelatin has dissolved. Stir in the cold water. Pour the liquid into a bundt pan, and refrigerate for 30 minutes or until slightly thickened.
2. Gently fold in the crushed pineapple. Refrigerate for 3 to 4 hours until the mixture is mostly solid.
3. In a bowl, whisk together the other 3-ounce package of gelatin and the remaining 1 cup boiling water until the gelatin has dissolved. Stir in the yogurt. Pour the mixture into the bundt pan over the pineapple gelatin, and refrigerate for 2 hours or until set.
4. Dip the bottom of the bundt pan into warm water. Place a plate on top of the pan, and invert the pan to remove the gelatin mold.

CLAMP

APPETIZERS

Now, I know what you're thinking—isn't *appetizer* just another word for *snack*? You'd be forgiven for thinking so, but it's not the same thing, and I'm going to tell you why. A snack, now, that's for one person. It's a solitary affair. Now, an appetizer? That's not simply for a man who wants a little bit more heft than your average snack provides; it's for a man who has to do some entertaining. That was the pitch I put together for the expandable Peltzer Party Platter back in '81. Sold enough units to completely remodel the kitchen! - RAND

HATCHING COCOONS (GF)

Your father pointed out that the cocoons that hatched the little green Christmas monsters were egg shaped. And since those little devils came out of them, he wondered, does that make them deviled eggs? (These are the kind of things he thinks of when he is not puttering away in his workshop, which might be why I convince him to keep inventing.) Now, even though the joke was silly, he was not wrong—those cocoons did look like eggs, and they certainly hatched little devils. All in all, it inspired a different way to make real deviled eggs. (They would be perfect for a big Halloween party, wouldn't they?) —Lynn

PREP TIME: 30 minutes (plus 6 hours of refrigeration)
COOK TIME: 12 minutes
YIELD: 6 servings
DIFFICULTY: Easy

INGREDIENTS

Dye
4 cups lukewarm water
1 tablespoon green food coloring

Bacon
2 bacon slices, uncooked

Eggs
6 large eggs
3 tablespoons mayonnaise
1 tablespoon diced sweet pickles
1 teaspoon yellow mustard
⅛ teaspoon hot smoked paprika
⅛ teaspoon kosher salt
⅛ teaspoon black pepper

DIRECTIONS

1. To make the dye: In a large bowl, whisk together the water and green food coloring. Set aside.
2. To make the bacon: In a skillet over medium-high heat, cook the bacon for 8 to 10 minutes until crispy. Let drain on paper towels. Dice into small pieces, and set aside.
3. To make the eggs: Place the eggs into a large saucepan, and cover with 1 to 2 inches of water. Turn the heat to medium-high, and bring the water to a boil.
4. Turn off the heat, cover with a lid, and let sit for 10 to 12 minutes.
5. Remove the eggs, and place into an ice bath for 15 minutes.
6. Gently roll the eggs in a towel to create cracks in the shells. Place the eggs into the green-dyed water, and refrigerate for 6 hours.
7. Peel the eggs. Slice a small amount off the bottom of the eggs so they stand upright. Slice off the top third of the eggs, setting aside the whites and placing the yolks into a medium bowl.
8. To the yolks, add the mayonnaise, sweet pickles, mustard, paprika, salt, and pepper. Stir until just combined. Place the mixture into a piping bag, and pipe onto the egg whites, covering the top of the egg. Top the eggs with diced bacon. Refrigerate until ready to serve.

½ QT
16oz
12oz
1 CUP
1 CUP
8oz

ROCKIN' RICKY RIALTO WHIPPED FETA (GF, V)

I have learned three things about Rockin' Ricky Rialto: First, he won't answer to anyone who does not call him "Rockin' Ricky," which I think is strange. But he is a radio personality, and I suppose it is normal for them to be strange. Second, he wears the loudest Hawaiian shirts I have ever seen on a person! And finally, he knows how to make this amazing appetizer. Rockin' Ricky brought this to a charity potluck once and was so over the moon from all the praise that the next day he told everyone the recipe right on his show. —Lynn

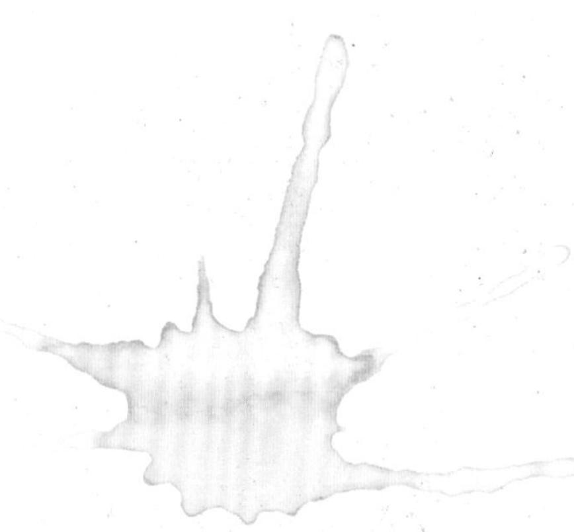

PREP TIME: 10 minutes
COOK TIME: N/A
YIELD: 6 servings
DIFFICULTY: Easy

INGREDIENTS

8-ounce feta cheese block, drained
¾ cup Greek yogurt
1 tablespoon lemon juice
1 tablespoon lemon zest
1 garlic clove
¼ teaspoon kosher salt
1 tablespoon extra virgin olive oil, plus more for serving
½ teaspoon freshly ground black pepper
1 tablespoon chopped fresh mint
1 tablespoon chopped fresh parsley
Pita chips, for serving

DIRECTIONS

1. Place the feta, Greek yogurt, lemon juice, lemon zest, garlic, and salt into a food processor. While slowly drizzling in the olive oil, pulse until creamy.
2. Spoon into a serving dish. Sprinkle with black pepper, top with mint and parsley, and drizzle with olive oil.
3. Serve with pita chips.

MOGWAI PUFFS (V)

I know this is a little tongue-in-cheek, but do you remember those fried green olives that I make for the neighborhood potlucks, the ones with the oregano? They have always been such a big hit. Lately I have been thinking about selling them at the Kingston Falls Christmas Market, but I thought they might need a better name. "Fried green olives" does not exactly stand out, after all. And then I thought, you know, they are a bit like mogwai, in a way—a little bit brown on the outside and a little bit green on the inside. Voilà, a new name: Mogwai Puffs! That will grab some attention, don't you think? —*Lynn*

PREP TIME: 15 minutes
COOK TIME: 10 minutes
YIELD: 15 servings
DIFFICULTY: Easy

INGREDIENTS

½ cup all-purpose flour
½ teaspoon kosher salt
¼ teaspoon black pepper
2 large eggs, beaten
1 cup panko breadcrumbs
1 teaspoon dried basil
1 teaspoon dried oregano
1 teaspoon onion powder
16 ounces extra-large green Spanish olives stuffed with garlic
2 cups vegetable oil, for frying

DIRECTIONS

1. Set up a breading station with three shallow dishes. In the first dish, whisk together the flour, salt, and pepper. Add the eggs to the second dish. In the third, stir together the breadcrumbs, basil, oregano, and onion powder. Set aside.
2. Drain the olives, and pat dry. Dredge the olives in the flour, shaking off the excess. Then dip them into the egg mixture and coat them in the breadcrumb mixture.
3. In a large saucepan over medium-high heat, heat the oil. Fry the olives in two batches for 1 to 2 minutes until golden brown. Let drain on a wire rack.

EXCESSIVE ONION DIP (GF, V)

Think about onions: They don't deserve a bad reputation just because they can make you cry—no, no, no. They're good for you. They strengthen your bones. Why, a person should have as many onions as they possibly can, which is why I've been working on an advanced tearless onion chopper to make this vegetable even easier to add to your diet. Think of it—you get into the kitchen, stare that onion right in the face, and chop it any way you want it. The only tears you'll cry are tears of joy over the fact that you can have your onion without stinging eyes. This could be the most exciting patent in the Peltzer portfolio since the Smokeless Ashtray! It'd make onions more accessible for soups and salads everywhere. Or, if you're about to sit down in front of a big game, your potato chips will never find a better partner than a good onion dip. - RAND

PREP TIME: 15 minutes
COOK TIME: 25 minutes
YIELD: 6 servings
DIFFICULTY: Easy

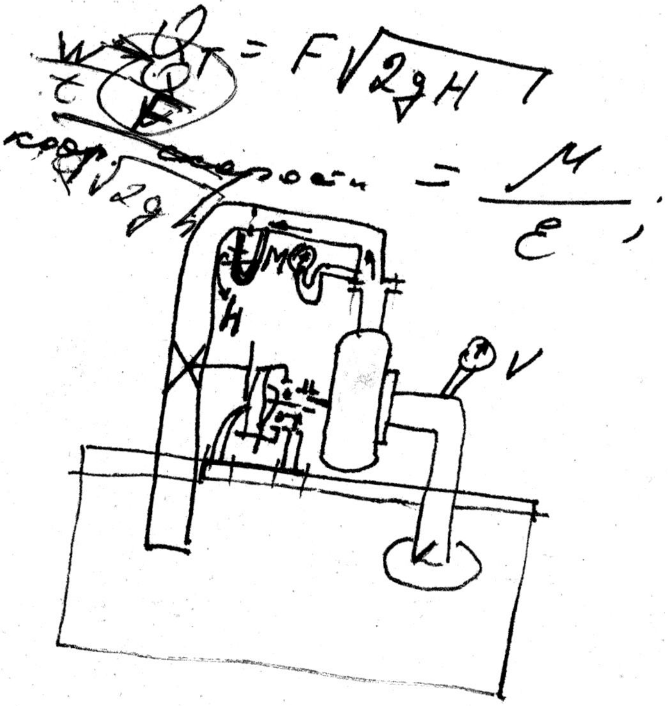

INGREDIENTS

1 tablespoon olive oil
1 large yellow onion, diced
1 cup sour cream
½ cup Greek yogurt
2 tablespoons fresh parsley, minced
½ teaspoon garlic powder
½ teaspoon onion powder
½ teaspoon kosher salt
¼ teaspoon black pepper
1 tablespoon fresh chives, minced

DIRECTIONS

1. In a medium skillet over medium heat, heat the olive oil. Add the onion, and cook for 25 minutes, stirring intermittently, until browned and caramelized. Let cool slightly.
2. In a medium bowl, stir together the sour cream, Greek yogurt, parsley, garlic powder, onion powder, salt, and pepper. Stir in the caramelized onions.
3. Top with chives. Refrigerate until ready to serve.

ARTICHOKE-POWERED APPETIZER (GF, V)

The humble artichoke might be the most underrated member of the vegetable kingdom. In fact, if you ask me, I'd say that the artichoke shows a lot of heart (get it?) and has a broad potential that goes far beyond just the culinary. I myself started to experiment with artichokes just a few years ago, and I discovered a whole slew of unexpected uses—including making it the principal component in a revolutionary new fully portable, plant-based sound system that will make all the Christmas lists once it's perfected. The perfecting part takes a lot of artichokes, though, which means they tend to pile up a bit in the workshop . . . . – RAND

PREP TIME: 10 minutes
COOK TIME: 20 minutes
YIELD: 6 servings
DIFFICULTY: Easy

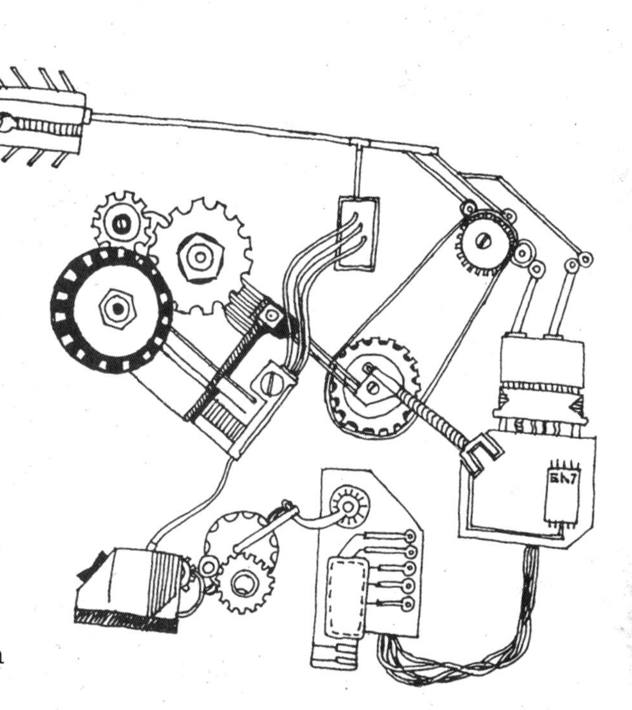

INGREDIENTS

Two 14-ounce cans quartered artichoke hearts, drained
1½ tablespoons olive oil
1 garlic clove, minced
1 teaspoon lemon pepper
½ teaspoon kosher salt
2 tablespoons feta cheese

DIRECTIONS

1. Preheat the oven to 425°F. Line a baking sheet with parchment paper.
2. Pat the artichokes dry, and place them in a large bowl. Toss with olive oil, garlic, lemon pepper, and salt.
3. Place the artichokes onto the prepped baking sheet, and top with feta cheese.
4. Bake for 20 minutes until golden brown.

GRETA'S MIDNIGHT KISSES (GF)

Between tending bar at Dorry's in Kingston Falls and showing New York City tourists around the Clamp Centre, I've seen some strange and unforgettable things. Some of those incidents involve people, because people are always strange. (And I've met some strange people—don't mention Lincoln around me!) Some of those incidents involve little green monsters that act like the strangest kind of people. What I'd never seen—until the gremlins invaded the Clamp Centre, anyway—was a full-on, almost spontaneous musical set piece. This was a performance right out of 1950s Hollywood, with props and this lady gremlin in a fancy evening dress whose lips looked like . . . well, like garlic knots or something. You couldn't look away. —Kate

PREP TIME: 30 minutes (plus 2 ½ hours for rising)
COOK TIME: 15 minutes
YIELD: 32 bread knots
DIFFICULTY: Moderate

INGREDIENTS

Dough

1 cup whole milk (warmed to 110°F)
2¼ teaspoons active dry yeast
2 tablespoons unsalted butter, melted
1 tablespoon granulated sugar
2½ cups bread flour
1 teaspoon kosher salt
1 tablespoon olive oil

Butter

6 tablespoons unsalted butter
4 garlic cloves, minced
3 tablespoons minced fresh parsley
½ teaspoon kosher salt
½ cup Parmesan cheese

(continued on page 38)

DIRECTIONS

1. To make the dough: In the bowl of a stand mixer fitted with the dough hook, stir together the milk, yeast, butter, and sugar. Let sit for 10 minutes until the yeast starts to bubble.
2. With the mixer on low, gradually add the flour and salt until just combined. With the speed on medium, knead the dough for 5 minutes until it is smooth and elastic.
3. Place the dough into a large bowl greased with olive oil, and cover with plastic wrap. Let the dough rise for 1½ hours until it has doubled in size.
4. Punch down the dough. Onto a lightly floured surface, knead it for 1 to 2 minutes; then divide it into 32 portions. Roll each piece into a snake shape, and tie each piece into a knot.
5. Place the knots 2 inches apart on the parchment-lined baking sheet. Cover with a tea towel, and let rise for another 1 hour.
6. To make the butter: In a small saucepan over medium heat, add the butter and garlic, and cook until the butter has melted. Stir in the parsley and salt.
7. Preheat the oven to 375°F.
8. Brush the dough with half of the butter mixture. Bake for 15 minutes until the knots are lightly browned.
9. Brush the remaining butter mixture onto the warm bread knots. Sprinkle with Parmesan, and serve.

GRANDPA FRED'S OCTOPUS APPETIZER

Way before he was promoted to a high-profile anchor job on the Clamp News Network, Grandpa Fred was my favorite horror movie host. I loved visiting the set of his show or grabbing lunch with him. He always had the best stories, which is part of what made him such a great host. Fred introduced his audience to some of the cheesiest monster movies ever made, but he made it fun. *Attack of the Octopus People* was the last movie he hosted before his promotion to the news desk, and in honor of that, I dug up a recipe for some tasty fried calamari. (Mom's not the only one who can be cheeky!) —Billy

PREP TIME: 10 minutes
COOK TIME: 9 minutes
YIELD: 8 servings
DIFFICULTY: Easy

INGREDIENTS

1 pound cleaned calamari, both rings and tentacles
1 cup buttermilk
1 teaspoon garlic powder
1 teaspoon onion powder
¼ teaspoon hot smoked paprika
1 cup all-purpose flour
½ cup cornstarch
1 teaspoon kosher salt
½ teaspoon lemon pepper
2 cups vegetable oil
1 teaspoon seasoned salt
2 teaspoons chopped fresh parsley

DIRECTIONS

1. In a large bowl, combine the calamari, buttermilk, garlic powder, onion powder, and paprika.
2. In a shallow dish, whisk together the flour, cornstarch, salt, and lemon pepper. Remove the calamari from the buttermilk mixture, and dredge in the seasoned flour.
3. In a large saucepan, heat the oil to 375°F. Working in batches, fry the calamari for 2 to 3 minutes until golden brown. Drain on a wire rack.
4. Sprinkle with seasoned salt and parsley, and serve.

HIGH-VOLTAGE CHEESE (V)

The Splice o' Life, the genetics lab on the fifty-first floor of the Clamp Centre, was the weirdest place in the building. And it wasn't because the guy in charge, Dr. Catheter, reminded me of Dracula, or that he had a weird obsession with diseases, or even that I couldn't tell whether his assistants, Martin and Lewis, were twins or some kind of lab experiment themselves. It was that they fed their lab rats a specialized diet of electrified cheese. Who does that? I don't know what else they might've done to that cheese, but I know that it looked neat and smelled delicious. This baked Brie was as close as I could get without advanced technology on my side.

–Billy

PREP TIME: 15 minutes
COOK TIME: 30 minutes
YIELD: 12 servings
DIFFICULTY: Easy

INGREDIENTS

1 puff pastry sheet, thawed
8-ounce Brie cheese wheel
¼ cup cherry jam
¼ cup chopped hazelnuts, plus more for garnish
1 tablespoon honey
¼ teaspoon kosher salt
1 sprig fresh rosemary, plus more for garnish
1 large egg, beaten, plus 1 tablespoon water, for egg wash
Crackers, for serving (optional)

DIRECTIONS

1. Preheat the oven to 375°F. Prep a pie plate with nonstick cooking spray.
2. Roll out the puff pastry, and place the Brie in the center. Spread the cherry jam evenly on top. Sprinkle with the hazelnuts, drizzle with honey, and then sprinkle with salt. Place the rosemary in the center as a garnish.
3. Starting with one corner, wrap and pleat the puff pastry, encasing the Brie. Brush with egg wash. Use a knife to make small vents around the pastry.
4. Bake for 25 to 30 minutes until golden brown.
5. Add more rosemary and hazelnuts around the edge of the pie plate, for garnish. Let cool slightly, and serve with crackers.

DANGER
HIGH
VOLTAGE

CLAMP
PREMIERE REGENCY TRADE CENTRE
& RETAIL CONCOURSE
250
APPROX
500
APPROX
400
300
200
Karter
500
APPROX
GG-17
500ml
400
300

VEGETABLE MEDLEY (GF, V, V+)

Of all the weird mutations that were caused after the gremlins exposed themselves to gene-altering materials from the Splice o' Life research labs, the most unexpected mutation was the one that transformed one gremlin from a singular animal to a medley of vegetables, like a walking jar of pickled veggies. Sometimes when I pass a salad bar, I wonder—would the veggie gremlin have thrived on sunlight like a plant does, or would it have melted him into a giant pile of pico de gallo? I guess it's like the old horror movies used to say: Some things we were never meant to know. At least, I hope we're never meant to find that out. —Billy

PREP TIME: 15 minutes (plus 24 hours of refrigeration)
COOK TIME: N/A
YIELD: 12 servings
DIFFICULTY: Easy

INGREDIENTS

1 cup cherry tomatoes
1 cup green beans
½ cup sliced carrots
2 garlic cloves, crushed
1 teaspoon black peppercorns
½ teaspoon mustard seeds
2 sprigs fresh dill
1 cup hot water
1 cup champagne vinegar
1 tablespoon kosher salt
1 teaspoon granulated sugar

DIRECTIONS

1. Into a large glass mason jar, add the tomatoes, green beans, carrots, garlic, peppercorns, mustard seeds, and dill.
2. In a small bowl, stir together the hot water, champagne vinegar, salt, and sugar. Pour the liquid over the ingredients in the jar. Let cool completely.
3. Seal the jar with the lid. Refrigerate for 24 hours before serving.

MAIN DISHES

Now, I've always liked a big meal myself, and not just because I have a big appetite. No, I've always enjoyed these because, with the time you have over several courses, you can take proper measure of whoever it is you're breaking bread with. I can tell you now, I've sold almost as much inventory over a good dinner as I have after making the rounds at any given convention. People tend to be more open while eating, and that's a fact—but it doesn't hurt to have the right food in front of them, either. This section is full of main dishes, the centerpieces of the kind of big-deal meals a young individual like yourself might be expected to plan—whether it's a business dinner with the kind of company that deserves better than pizza, a family supper, or any special occasion you could care to name! - RAND

HEALING CHICKEN SOUP

This cookbook has been a such fun project—and very therapeutic, in the way it turned those scary little monsters into the inspiration for not-so-scary recipes . . . but I have truly always believed in the healing power of food, which is why this recipe is so very important to me. Sweetheart, I want you (and Kate!) to be healthy and happy, and a big bowl of chicken soup guarantees that. Do not laugh! It is good for what ails you, as my grandpa always said. Whether it is a little cold or a lot of stress, this soup will help. I promise! –Lynn

PREP TIME: 25 minutes
COOK TIME: 2 hours
YIELD: 10 servings
DIFFICULTY: Moderate

INGREDIENTS

Broth

8-piece fryer chicken
1 onion, peeled and quartered
2 carrots, peeled and chopped
2 celery ribs, chopped
½ cup torn cilantro
2 garlic cloves
1 tablespoon kosher salt
1 teaspoon black peppercorns
1 bay leaf
10 cups water

Soup

1 tablespoon olive oil
1 large onion, diced
2 large carrots, peeled and diced
2 celery ribs, diced
2 garlic cloves, minced
1 teaspoon kosher salt
½ teaspoon black pepper
1 tablespoon fresh rosemary
1 tablespoon fresh thyme
½ teaspoon turmeric
6 ounces egg noodles
Chopped fresh parsley, for garnish

DIRECTIONS

1. To make the broth: To a large stock pot over medium-high heat, add the chicken, onion, carrots, celery, cilantro, garlic, salt, peppercorns, bay leaf, and water. Bring to a boil. Cover, and reduce heat. Simmer for 1 hour and 30 minutes.
2. Strain the broth, and set aside.
3. Shred the chicken, discarding the bones and skin. Set aside.
4. To make the soup: In a large Dutch oven, heat the olive oil. Add the onion, carrots, and celery. Cook for 4 to 5 minutes until the vegetables have softened.
5. Stir in the garlic, salt, pepper, rosemary, thyme, and turmeric.
6. Pour in the strained broth, and bring to a boil. Add the egg noodles, and cook for 10 minutes until they are al dente.
7. Stir in the shredded chicken. Cover, reduce heat to low, and simmer for 10 minutes.
8. Sprinkle with parsley, and serve.

ROASTED GREMLIN CHOPS (GF)

This pork chop recipe was an old favorite of my father's—and something you might want to know how to make for a special occasion (like an anniversary—Mom made this for Dad every year!). And you know, now that I think about it, thanks to the gremolata sauce, this recipe even neatly fits in with my gremlin theme—although I cannot decide whether it fits because gremolata is green or because it starts with the same letters as gremlin. My, what a coincidence! —Lynn

PREP TIME: 20 minutes (plus 3 hours of refrigeration)
COOK TIME: 15 minutes
YIELD: 2 servings
DIFFICULTY: Moderate

INGREDIENTS

Brine

6 cups hot water
¼ cup packed light brown sugar
¼ cup kosher salt
2 garlic cloves, smashed
1 tablespoon peppercorns
½ teaspoon whole cloves
1 sprig fresh rosemary
2 bone-in center-cut pork chops

Gremolata

½ bunch fresh flat-leaf parsley, minced
Zest of 1 lemon
1 garlic clove, minced
1 tablespoon extra-virgin olive oil
1 tablespoon lemon juice
½ teaspoon kosher salt

Pork Chops

1 tablespoon light brown sugar
2 teaspoons smoked paprika
1 teaspoon cumin
1 teaspoon garlic powder
1 teaspoon onion powder
½ teaspoon chili powder
¼ teaspoon black pepper
2 tablespoons olive oil

(continued on page 50)

YOUR MOTHER MAKES ME THESE PORK CHOPS FOR MY BIRTHDAY-AND THEY ARE SO GOOD, I DON'T EVEN HAVE AN INVENTION THAT COULD IMPROVE THEM! THIS RECIPE WILL BE THE GIFT THAT KEEPS ON GIVING. NOW, IF YOU WANT MY ADVICE, DON'T SAVE THEM FOR A SPECIAL OCCASION. YOU PUT THEM INTO THE REGULAR ROTATION! - RAND

DIRECTIONS

1. To make the brine: In a large bowl, whisk together the hot water, brown sugar, and salt until dissolved.
2. Stir in the garlic, peppercorns, and cloves.
3. Place the brine into a sealable container, and add the fresh rosemary and pork chops. Refrigerate for 3 hours.
4. To make the gremolata: In a small bowl, stir together the minced parsley, lemon zest, garlic, olive oil, lemon juice, and salt. Set aside.
5. To make the pork chops: Remove the pork chops, and discard the brine. Rinse, and pat dry.
6. In a small bowl, stir together the brown sugar, paprika, cumin, garlic powder, onion powder, chili powder, and pepper. Press the mixture into the pork chops on both sides.
7. In a skillet over medium-high heat, heat the olive oil. Cook the pork chops for 2 minutes on each side until browned.
8. Turn down the heat to medium-low, cover, and cook the pork chops for an additional 5 to 10 minutes or until an internal thermometer reads 145°F.
9. Cover with foil to tent, and let rest for 10 minutes.
10. Top the pork chops with gremolata, and serve.

CHRISTMAS HAM (GF)

Even with everything that happened during Christmas a few years ago, I still love that holiday and all the traditions that come with it—especially the food. I believe that making a big holiday meal and bringing family and friends together to enjoy it is always one of the best parts of the year . . . and for the centerpiece of the dinner, I have always preferred a Christmas ham. You know, your father tried for many years to argue that turkey was the proper entrée for both Thanksgiving and Christmas, and that ham should stick to Easter . . . but if you look closely, you will notice that the recipe I am adding to this book for you does not come with drumsticks, so you can see how well he convinced me. —Lynn

PREP TIME: 10 minutes
COOK TIME: 2 hours 10 minutes
YIELD: 10 servings
DIFFICULTY: Easy

INGREDIENTS

8-pound bone-in ham
¾ cup light brown sugar
1 tablespoon smoked paprika
1 teaspoon kosher salt
1 teaspoon black pepper
1 tablespoon Dijon mustard
Two 12-ounce cans cola

DIRECTIONS

1. Preheat the oven to 325°F. Line a 9-by-13-by-4-inch baking pan with heavy aluminum foil. Place the ham into the pan.
2. In a small bowl, whisk together the brown sugar, paprika, salt, and pepper. Stir in the Dijon mustard and 1 to 2 tablespoons cola.
3. Brush the brown sugar paste over the ham. Pour the remaining cola into the bottom of the pan.
4. Cover with tented foil, and cook for 1½ hours, basting every 20 minutes.
5. Remove the foil, and cook for another 40 minutes, continuing to baste. Cook until an internal thermometer reads 145°F.
6. Let rest for 15 minutes before slicing.

FIVE-EGG OMELET (GF, V)

You remember the Peltzer Egg Cracker 5000—it was always a little bit too good at its job, and no amount of adjusting could slow it down. Sounds like the start of a joke, doesn't it? An inventor complaining that his invention works too well! But here's a life lesson for you, son, and it's a valuable one—there is no accident or error that can't also lead to opportunity. I believe that, and that's what this recipe is. If you have some cracked eggs handy, what do you do? You make an omelet. And when you have as many cracked eggs on hand as we do after the Egg Cracker does its thing, you make a really big omelet. It makes one heck of a brunch offering, let me tell you. - RAND

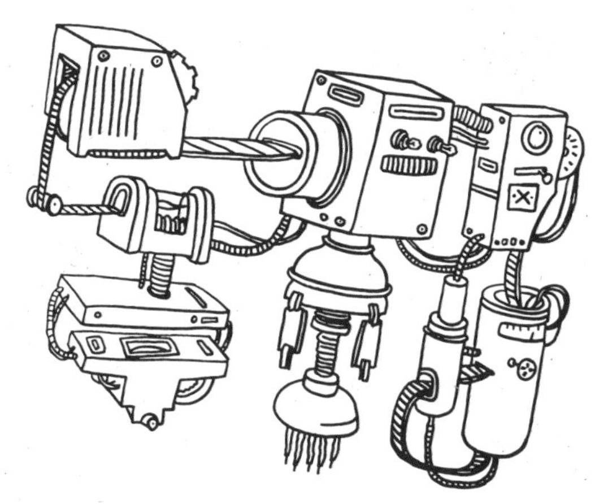

PREP TIME: 5 minutes
COOK TIME: 10 minutes
YIELD: 3 servings
DIFFICULTY: Moderate

INGREDIENTS

Mushrooms

1 tablespoon unsalted butter
4 ounces sliced mushrooms
1 tablespoon minced shallot
½ teaspoon dried basil
⅛ teaspoon black pepper

Eggs

5 large eggs
½ teaspoon kosher salt
2 tablespoons unsalted butter, divided, plus more to finish
½ cup spinach
¼ cup feta cheese
1 tablespoon chopped fresh parsley

DIRECTIONS

1. To make the mushrooms: In a small skillet over medium-high heat, melt the butter. Add the mushrooms and shallot, and cook for 5 to 6 minutes until softened. Add the basil and black pepper. Cook for 1 to 2 minutes more. Remove to a bowl, and set aside.
2. To make the eggs: In a large bowl, whisk together the eggs and salt.
3. In a large skillet over medium-high heat, melt 1 tablespoon of the butter. Pour in the eggs, stirring with a spatula.
4. Add the mushrooms, spinach, and feta cheese into the middle of the eggs.
5. As the edges of the omelet form, use a spatula to loosen them. Fold over the omelet. Brush with the remaining butter.
6. Sprinkle with parsley, and serve.

KATE'S COMFORT PB&J (V)

Whenever I get stressed out, the only thing that can pull me together is the right kind of comfort food—and the right kind is a peanut butter and jelly sandwich. This recipe reminds me of the PB&J phase I went through as a kid, but it also reminds me of a terrible, horrible memory of Lincoln's birthday at the park. This man . . . he had a beard and a hat . . . oh, god . . . not as horrible a memory as the one I have for Christmas, but just thinking of it stresses me out more than a gremlin in a raincoat. —*Kate*

PREP TIME: 15 minutes
COOK TIME: 4 minutes
YIELD: 1 serving
DIFFICULTY: Moderate

INGREDIENTS

1 tablespoon whipped cream cheese, softened
2 slices brioche
2 tablespoons peanut butter
2 tablespoons blackberry jam
½ cup thinly sliced green apple
1 large egg
2 tablespoons heavy whipping cream
¼ teaspoon cinnamon
⅛ teaspoon kosher salt
1 tablespoon unsalted butter

DIRECTIONS

1. Spread the cream cheese onto one slice of bread. Top with peanut butter.
2. Onto the other slice of bread, spread the jam. Layer the apple slices.
3. Bring the two sides together to form a sandwich.
4. In a shallow dish, whisk together the egg, heavy whipping cream, cinnamon, and salt.
5. In a skillet over medium-high heat, melt the butter.
6. Dip the sandwich into the egg mixture, to coat. Place the sandwich into the pan, and cook on both sides for 1 to 2 minutes until golden brown.
7. Serve immediately.

SECRETARY'S SNAPPY SANDWICH (V)

Mr. Clamp's secretary, Betty, told me about this sandwich she liked for lunch. She said that it had some bite to it, which sounded delicious. I went to the deli she orders from, but to be honest, their sandwiches weren't as impressive as she made them sound . . . so I added a few things to spice it up. I mentioned my improvements to Betty the next time I saw her, and do you know what she said? That I heard only half the story, which was actually about how some big lizard put a mousetrap in her sandwich, so it felt like the sandwich was biting her! Just goes to show, sometimes you need to let people finish their stories . . . . –Kate

PREP TIME: 15 minutes
COOK TIME: 10 minutes
YIELD: 1 serving
DIFFICULTY: Moderate

INGREDIENTS

Mushrooms

½ cup all-purpose flour
½ teaspoon garlic powder
½ teaspoon onion powder
½ teaspoon smoked paprika
½ teaspoon kosher salt, plus more for sprinkling
¼ teaspoon black pepper
¼ teaspoon cayenne powder
½ cup whole milk
4 ounces oyster mushrooms
2 cups vegetable oil

Sandwich

2 slices sourdough bread
1 slice Swiss cheese
2 romaine lettuce leaves
1 thinly sliced tomato
¼ cup kimchi

DIRECTIONS

1. To make the mushrooms: In a medium bowl, whisk together the flour, garlic powder, onion powder, paprika, salt, pepper, and cayenne.
2. Make a well in the center of the dry ingredients, and whisk in the milk until the mixture is smooth.
3. Dip the mushrooms in the batter, to coat.
4. In a large saucepan, heat the oil over medium-high heat to 350°F. Fry the mushrooms for 3 to 4 minutes until golden brown. Let drain on a wire rack. Sprinkle with kosher salt.
5. To make the sandwich: Toast the bread, and top one slice with cheese. Toast again for 3 to 4 minutes, until the cheese has melted.
6. Onto the cheese toast, place first the lettuce and then the mushrooms. Add the tomato and kimchi. Top with the second piece of toasted bread, and serve.

MICROWAVE
WITH
Marge

TUNA NOODLE CHEESE PRODUCT CHOWDER SURPRISE

Clamp Cable Network's *Microwave with Marge* was the kind of comfort TV you would watch after having a nightmare about the time in ninth grade when you were supposed to dissect a frog, but you thought it was still alive and judging you, and you couldn't get back to sleep without something to calm you down . . . . This microwave-less version of Marge's classic dish isn't as fast, but it's just as comforting, so it's a must-have recipe if those gremlins ever wreak havoc—or when another horrible memory crops up again. –Kate

PREP TIME: 20 minutes
COOK TIME: 50 minutes
YIELD: 10 servings
DIFFICULTY: Easy

INGREDIENTS

Casserole
8 ounces egg noodles
3 tablespoons unsalted butter, divided
½ cup diced onion
1 celery rib, diced
2 garlic cloves, minced
8 ounces white mushrooms, sliced
¼ cup all-purpose flour
1 cup whole milk
1 cup heavy whipping cream
1 teaspoon dried thyme
½ teaspoon onion powder
½ teaspoon kosher salt
¼ teaspoon nutmeg
¼ teaspoon black pepper
Two 5-ounce cans tuna, drained
¾ cup frozen peas, thawed

Topping
⅓ cup panko breadcrumbs
3 tablespoons unsalted butter, melted
1 cup shredded cheddar cheese

(continued on page 60)

DIRECTIONS

1. Preheat the oven to 400°F. Prep a 9-by-13-inch baking dish with nonstick cooking spray; set aside.
2. To make the casserole: Bring a large pot of water to a boil. Add the egg noodles, and cook for 8 to 9 minutes until they are al dente. Drain, but do not rinse. Set aside.
3. In the same pot over medium heat, melt 1 tablespoon of the butter. Add the onion, celery, and garlic. Cook for 4 to 5 minutes until the vegetables have softened.
4. Add the mushrooms, and cook for 3 to 4 more minutes until softened. Remove, and set aside.
5. Into the same pot, over medium-high heat, add the remaining 2 tablespoons of butter. Whisk in the flour, and cook for 2 to 3 minutes until cooked through. Whisk in the milk and heavy whipping cream.
6. Cook for 4 to 5 minutes to thicken the mixture. Stir in the thyme, onion powder, salt, nutmeg, and pepper.
7. Turn off the heat, and stir in the noodles, mushrooms, tuna, and peas.
8. Pour the mixture into the prepped baking dish. Bake for 20 minutes until lightly browned.
9. To make the topping: In a small bowl, stir together the panko and butter. Spread evenly on top of the casserole, and sprinkle on the shredded cheese.
10. Bake for an additional 5 minutes until golden brown.

DON'T GET IT WET BURRITO

When I decided to add this recipe to the book, it was because I really love a good burrito. They're practically all I ate my junior year of high school (but one of the worst things to eat over an in-progress art project). Unfortunately, our experiences with gremlins now make me think twice whenever I see the word wet. I doubt that the second rule of mogwai care—never get them wet—also applies to a wet burrito, but I can't be 100 percent sure. Either way, it's best to be careful and watch out for mogwai when preparing these burritos. —*Billy*

PREP TIME: 25 minutes
COOK TIME: 40 minutes
YIELD: 6 servings
DIFFICULTY: Hard

INGREDIENTS

Sauce

6 tablespoons unsalted butter
6 tablespoons all-purpose flour
32 ounces beef broth
1 tablespoon tomato paste
2 tablespoons chili powder
1 teaspoon cumin
1 teaspoon garlic powder
1 teaspoon smoked paprika
½ teaspoon kosher salt

Meat

1 tablespoon olive oil
½ cup minced onion
2 garlic cloves, minced
2 pounds ground beef
1 tablespoon Worcestershire sauce
1½ tablespoons chili powder
1 tablespoon cumin
2 teaspoons garlic powder
2 teaspoons onion powder
1½ teaspoons oregano
½ teaspoon kosher salt
¼ teaspoon black pepper

Burritos

One 16-ounce can refried beans, divided
6 burrito-size flour tortillas,warmed
4 cups Mexican cheese, divided
2 tablespoons crema
1 tablespoon torn cilantro leaves

(continued on page 63)

DIRECTIONS

1. To make the sauce: In a large saucepan over medium heat, whisk together the butter and flour for 2 to 3 minutes until slightly golden.
2. Whisk in the beef broth, tomato paste, chili powder, cumin, garlic powder, paprika, and salt. Let simmer for 3 to 5 minutes until thickened. Remove from heat, and set aside.
3. To make the meat: In a skillet over medium-high heat, heat the olive oil. Add the onion and garlic, and cook for 4 to 5 minutes until softened.
4. Add the beef, and cook for 7 to 8 minutes until browned.
5. Stir in the Worcestershire sauce, chili powder, cumin, garlic powder, onion powder, oregano, salt, and pepper. Cook for 2 to 3 minutes until fragrant. Set aside.
6. To make the burritos: Preheat the oven to 400°F. Pour a third of the sauce into a 9-by-13-inch baking pan. Set aside.
7. Spread ¼ cup beans onto a tortilla. Add a sixth of the ground beef mixture. Top with ⅓ cup cheese. Roll up the burrito, and place it into the pan. Repeat with the remaining ingredients.
8. Pour the remaining sauce over the burritos. Top with the remaining 2 cups of cheese. Bake for 15 minutes until the cheese has melted.
9. Drizzle with crema, sprinkle with cilantro, and serve.

MIDNIGHT FRIED CHICKEN

Mogwai can be very different from what you'd expect. Gosh, just by looking at one, you'd never think their appetites were so big that they could power through a plate of fried chicken faster than a starving piranha. But I saw it happen. The bad part was, I saw it happen after midnight, which is the one time you don't want mogwai to be eating anything. That's the third rule of mogwai care—the most important one: Don't ever feed them after midnight. But for people, this fried chicken might be the perfect midnight snack. —Billy

PREP TIME: 15 minutes (plus 4 hours of refrigeration)
COOK TIME: 24 minutes
YIELD: 6 servings
DIFFICULTY: Moderate

INGREDIENTS

Buttermilk Marinade
2 cups buttermilk
2 eggs
¼ cup pickle juice
1 tablespoon hot sauce
1 teaspoon kosher salt
4 pounds whole chicken pieces

Dredge
1 cup all-purpose flour
½ cup cornstarch
1 tablespoon confectioners sugar
1 tablespoon garlic powder
1 tablespoon onion powder
2 teaspoons smoked paprika
2 teaspoons garlic salt
1 teaspoon white pepper
½ teaspoon cayenne pepper
4 cups vegetable oil

DIRECTIONS

1. To make the buttermilk marinade: In a sealable container, whisk together the buttermilk, eggs, pickle juice, hot sauce, and salt. Add the chicken. Cover, and refrigerate for 4 hours.
2. To make the dredge: In a sealable bag, add the flour, cornstarch, confectioners sugar, garlic powder, onion powder, paprika, garlic salt, white pepper, and cayenne.
3. Remove the chicken, and discard the marinade. Dredge the chicken pieces in the flour mixture.
4. In a large Dutch oven, heat the oil over medium-high heat to 350°F.
5. Add the chicken to the Dutch oven, and fry in batches for 10 to 12 minutes on each side until golden brown and an internal thermometer reads 160°F. Let drain on a wire rack.

MURRAY'S MEATLOAF

If there's one thing the Futtermans have always loved, it's meatloaf. In fact, Mr. Futterman loves meatloaf so much that even the smell of gremlins fried by high-voltage electricity reminded him of the meal. (Well, the smell reminded him of *burnt* meatloaf, but it's still the first place his mind went.) After Mrs. Futterman flipped through some of Mom's recipes in this book, she insisted on contributing Murray's favorite meatloaf recipe. It's a pretty neat meal that includes something from all the major food groups, which I didn't even think was possible, and it's a great reminder of how to get rid of those little pests. —*Billy*

PREP TIME: 20 minutes
COOK TIME: 1 hour 25 minutes
YIELD: 8 servings
DIFFICULTY: Moderate

INGREDIENTS

3 bacon slices, uncooked
½ cup diced onion
2 garlic cloves, minced
1 pound ground beef
1 pound ground pork
1 cup frozen spinach, well drained
½ cup breadcrumbs
1 large egg
⅓ cup whole milk
1 tablespoon Worcestershire sauce
1 teaspoon garlic powder
½ teaspoon onion powder
½ teaspoon ground mustard
½ teaspoon kosher salt
¼ teaspoon black pepper
¾ cup ketchup
¼ cup apricot jam
1 tablespoon chopped parsley, for garnish

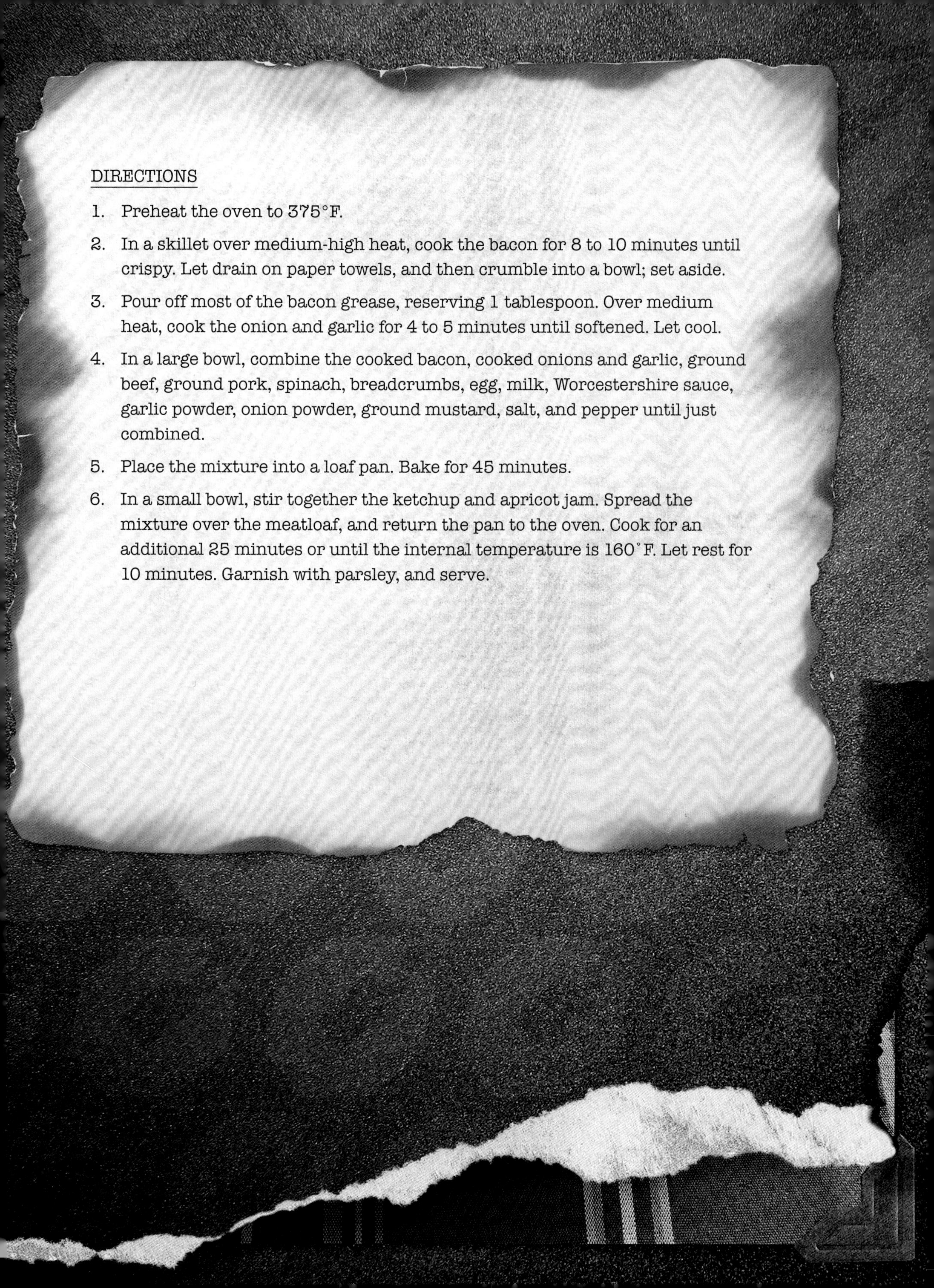

DIRECTIONS

1. Preheat the oven to 375°F.
2. In a skillet over medium-high heat, cook the bacon for 8 to 10 minutes until crispy. Let drain on paper towels, and then crumble into a bowl; set aside.
3. Pour off most of the bacon grease, reserving 1 tablespoon. Over medium heat, cook the onion and garlic for 4 to 5 minutes until softened. Let cool.
4. In a large bowl, combine the cooked bacon, cooked onions and garlic, ground beef, ground pork, spinach, breadcrumbs, egg, milk, Worcestershire sauce, garlic powder, onion powder, ground mustard, salt, and pepper until just combined.
5. Place the mixture into a loaf pan. Bake for 45 minutes.
6. In a small bowl, stir together the ketchup and apricot jam. Spread the mixture over the meatloaf, and return the pan to the oven. Cook for an additional 25 minutes or until the internal temperature is 160°F. Let rest for 10 minutes. Garnish with parsley, and serve.

CANADIAN CLEANED FISH

At what I'd like to once again stress was nothing more than a work-related dinner meeting, I had the chance to eat at what I'm told is a very chic Canadian restaurant. I had no idea what I was in for when it came to Canadian cuisine, but this place had a fish special that knocked my socks off. And what made the fish so good that it was the hot ticket on the menu? Maple syrup. Could anything be more Canadian than that? Maybe the chocolate "moose" they offered for dessert (page 94). —Billy

PREP TIME: 20 minutes (plus 20 minutes of refrigeration)
COOK TIME: 21 minutes
YIELD: 4 servings
DIFFICULTY: Easy

INGREDIENTS

¼ cup maple syrup
2 tablespoons tamari
1 tablespoon mirin (sweet Japanese rice wine)
2 garlic cloves, minced
1 teaspoon minced ginger
⅛ teaspoon ground black pepper
1 pound salmon filets

DIRECTIONS

1. In a small bowl, whisk together the maple syrup, tamari, mirin, garlic, ginger, and pepper.
2. In a sealable container, add the salmon filets and pour the marinade over the top. Refrigerate for 20 minutes.
3. Preheat the oven to 400°F. Line a baking sheet with foil.
4. Place the salmon filets onto the prepped pan. Discard the marinade.
5. Cook for 15 to 20 minutes or until an internal thermometer reads 135°F.
6. Broil for 1 minute until the top has caramelized. Serve immediately.

FROM THE OFFICE OF DANIEL CLAMP

TO: William Peltzer

FROM: Daniel Clamp

SUBJECT: Clamp's Shredded Salad (GF)

Bill—I was down in the art department and saw this charming little book on your desk. Recipes! Gremlins! Heartwarming family advice! I love it all, and I think we should talk about publishing. This could be a key item in the general store of the Clamp Corners project, don't you think? Give people a real introduction to small-town cuisine.

I've had my secretary attach a little offering of my own for this collection, to show what I could contribute to such a venture. And there's more where this came from, believe me! Let's set up a lunch soon, shall we? We'll hash all this out. In the meantime, enjoy the salad!

ATTACHED: Clamp's Shredded Salad (trademark pending)

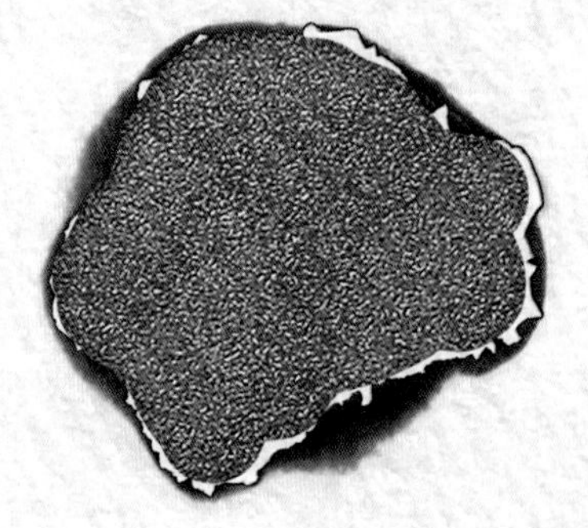

PREP TIME: 25 minutes

COOK TIME: N/A

YIELD: 8 servings

DIFFICULTY: Easy

INGREDIENTS

Dressing

¼ cup Japanese mayonnaise

1 tablespoon white miso

1 teaspoon rice vinegar

1½ teaspoons granulated sugar

½ teaspoon kosher salt

¼ teaspoon white pepper

Salad

1 head cabbage, shaved thin

5 ounces imitation crab, shredded

1 medium carrot, julienned

1 medium cucumber, julienned

1 green onion, diced

½ teaspoon black sesame seeds

DIRECTIONS

1. To make the dressing: In a small bowl, stir together the Japanese mayonnaise, white miso, rice vinegar, sugar, salt, and pepper. Set aside.
2. To make the salad: Soak the shaved cabbage in a large bowl of ice water for 15 minutes. Drain, and dry thoroughly.
3. In a large bowl, toss the cabbage, crab, carrot, and cucumber.
4. Top with dressing, sprinkle with diced green onions and sesame seeds, and serve.

DESSERTS

There's nothing more versatile than a dessert, and I'm going to tell you why. Say, for the sake of argument, that you've just had a day that really got to you, wore you right down. You need something to make you feel a little better—a dessert will fix you right up. Or take it from the other direction. You had a fantastic day, couldn't be better. You are on top of the world and looking to celebrate—grab yourself a treat. It can't miss, either way. . . well, not unless you misplaced your sweet tooth. - RAND

GREMLIN SCONES (V)

I always appreciate any excuse to have a fancy afternoon tea party with little sandwiches, and all the accoutrements. My favorite treats are scones. The last time my group got together, I was feeling a little impish and figured, why not put little gremlin faces on them? Our whole group had fun tearing them apart. Mr. Anderson even dunked his in the hot tea, which you should not do with scones—or with gremlins, come to think of it—but he got such a giggle fit out of it, I had to let it pass.

–Lynn

PREP TIME: 20 minutes
(plus 15 minutes of refrigeration)
COOK TIME: 18 minutes
YIELD: 9 scones
DIFFICULTY: Easy

INGREDIENTS

Scones

2¼ cups all-purpose flour
½ cup granulated sugar
1 tablespoon matcha powder
1 tablespoon baking powder
¼ teaspoon kosher salt
½ cup (1 stick) unsalted butter, melted
1 large egg
1 cup heavy cream
½ teaspoon vanilla extract

Icing

2½ cups confectioners sugar
1½ tablespoons meringue powder
3 tablespoons warm water
Black food coloring
Red food coloring
Yellow food coloring

DIRECTIONS

1. To make the scones: In a large bowl, whisk together the flour, sugar, matcha powder, baking powder, and salt.
2. Make a well in the center of the dry ingredients, and stir in the butter, egg, heavy cream, and vanilla until just combined. Refrigerate the dough for 15 minutes.
3. Preheat the oven to 400°F. Line two baking sheets with parchment paper.
4. Use two-thirds of the dough to create 9 rounds. Use the remaining third of the dough to create 3-inch long gremlin ears. Place the dough 2 inches apart on the prepped baking sheets. Bake for 18 minutes. Transfer to a wire rack to cool.
5. To make the icing: In a bowl with a hand mixer, stir together the confectioners sugar and meringue powder. Slowly add the water until the icing is combined. Add a teaspoon of water, if necessary, to get the right consistency.
6. Divide the icing into four small bowls. Leave one bowl as is. Into the second bowl, stir in the black food coloring to dye the icing black. Into the third bowl, stir in the red food coloring to dye the icing red. Finally, into the last bowl, stir in the yellow food coloring to dye the icing yellow. Place the icings into four separate piping bags.
7. Use icing to create face details. When the icing is dry, the scones are ready to serve.

KILLER GINGERBREAD COOKIES (V)

Christmastime holiday traditions are a wonderful thing. There is caroling, if you like to sing. Trimming a Christmas tree and unwrapping presents around that same tree with a warm drink in hand also build wonderful memories during the holidays. My favorite tradition, though, has always been baking gingerbread cookies. Did you know that, out of the thousands I have made, the only batch that never got to be enjoyed by friends and family was the one stolen by a gremlin? But he got what was coming to him for ruining my delicious cookies! —Lynn

PREP TIME: 25 minutes
COOK TIME: 12 minutes
YIELD: 16 cookies
DIFFICULTY: Moderate

INGREDIENTS

Cookies

3 cups all-purpose flour
2 teaspoons ground ginger
2 teaspoons cinnamon
½ teaspoon baking powder
½ teaspoon nutmeg
¼ teaspoon ground allspice
¼ teaspoon ground cloves
¼ teaspoon kosher salt
1 cup (2 sticks) unsalted butter, softened
1 cup light brown sugar
1 large egg
¼ cup dark molasses
1½ teaspoons vanilla extract

Icing

2½ cups confectioners sugar
1 tablespoon light corn syrup
½ teaspoon vanilla extract
2 tablespoons whole milk
Green food gel coloring
Red food gel coloring
Yellow food gel coloring

(continued on page 78)

DIRECTIONS

1. To make the cookies: In a medium bowl, whisk together the flour, ginger, cinnamon, baking powder, nutmeg, allspice, cloves, and salt. Set aside.
2. In the bowl of an electric mixer, cream together the butter and brown sugar until fluffy.
3. Stir in the egg, molasses, and vanilla until just combined.
4. Slowly add in the dry ingredients just until the dough comes together.
5. Split the dough into two, and wrap in plastic wrap. Chill in the refrigerator until you are ready to use.
6. Preheat the oven to 350°F. Line a baking sheet with parchment paper.
7. Roll out the dough to ¼ inch thick. Use a gingerbread man cookie cutter to cut out shapes.
8. Transfer the dough onto the prepped baking sheet.
9. Bake for 12 minutes, and then let cool on a wire rack.
10. To make the icing: In a small bowl, whisk together the confectioners sugar, corn syrup, vanilla, and milk until smooth.
11. Divide the icing equally among three small bowls. Use the food coloring to dye each bowl a different color.
12. Place the icing into piping bags, and decorate the cookies as desired.
13. When the icing is dry, the cookies are ready to serve.

MIDNIGHT SNACK CAKES (V)

When it comes to perfecting an invention, there are a lot of late nights in the ol' workshop. And you can't work all night on an empty stomach—that's why some genius out there came up with the midnight snack. I know what you're thinking—but just because a mogwai shouldn't eat after midnight doesn't mean that you need to hold back when your stomach starts rumbling. Now, for me, a deep-fried snack cake is the perfect choice. They call this "fair food" sometimes; I think that's because it's not fair to deny yourself—especially not when you've still got a night of work ahead. – RAND

PREP TIME: 15 minutes (plus 2 hours for freezing)
COOK TIME: 18 minutes
YIELD: 6 servings
DIFFICULTY: Moderate

INGREDIENTS

6 popsicle sticks
6 snack cakes
4 cups vegetable oil, for frying
1½ cups pancake mix
1 cup whole milk
½ teaspoon nutmeg
½ teaspoon kosher salt
1 tablespoon confectioners sugar, for garnish

DIRECTIONS

1. Insert the popsicle sticks two-thirds of the way into the ends of the snack cakes. Place on a parchment-lined baking sheet, and freeze for 2 hours.
2. In a large Dutch oven over medium-high heat, heat the oil to 350°F.
3. In a large bowl, whisk together the pancake mix, milk, nutmeg, and salt until smooth.
4. Dip the snack cakes into the batter, frying in batches for 2 to 3 minutes each until golden brown. Let cool on a wire rack.
5. Dust with confectioners sugar. Serve immediately.

KATE'S HATED HOLIDAY FRUITCAKE (V)

I've tried hard to get into the Christmas spirit, but there are just too many memories, too many terrible stories, too much baggage. There was the chimney incident, which traumatized me during childhood, in such a formative time. And then, just when I think I have enough of a handle on life to be able to enjoy a small part of the season again, I get trapped in Dorry's Tavern with a mob of tiny monsters that partied like it was the end of the world. The only thing I can do with all my feelings about this time of year is bake them into the biggest holiday cliché there is: a fruitcake. I mean, at least it makes the perfect gift! —Kate

PREP TIME: 20 minutes (plus 24 hours for soaking)
COOK TIME: 1 hour
YIELD: 10 servings
DIFFICULTY: Moderate

INGREDIENTS

Fruit
½ cup dried pineapple, diced
½ cup dried apricots, chopped
½ cup candied green cherries
½ cup candied red cherries
½ cup rum

Cake
1½ cups all-purpose flour
½ teaspoon baking powder
½ teaspoon cinnamon
¼ teaspoon allspice
¼ teaspoon nutmeg
¼ teaspoon kosher salt
½ cup (1 stick) unsalted butter, softened
1 cup packed light brown sugar
2 large eggs
¼ cup orange juice
½ teaspoon vanilla extract
½ cup chopped pecans
¼ cup candied ginger, diced
1 teaspoon lemon zest
1 teaspoon orange zest
⅓ cup apricot jam
1 tablespoon rum

Icing
1 cup confectioners sugar
1½ tablespoons whole milk
½ teaspoon lemon juice

Garnish
2 tablespoons whole cranberries
¼ cup whole pecans
1 tablespoon fresh rosemary sprigs
1 tablespoon confectioners sugar

(continued on page 83)

DIRECTIONS

1. To make the fruit: In a sealable bowl, toss the pineapple, apricots, green cherries, and red cherries with the rum. Cover the bowl, and let the fruit soak overnight.
2. To make the cake: Preheat the oven to 300°F. Prep a 9-by-5-inch loaf pan with parchment paper greased with nonstick spray.
3. In a medium bowl, whisk together the flour, baking powder, cinnamon, allspice, nutmeg, and salt. Set aside.
4. In the bowl of an electric mixer, cream together the butter and brown sugar for 2 to 3 minutes until fluffy. Stir in the eggs, orange juice, and vanilla.
5. Add the flour mixture until just combined.
6. Fold in the soaked fruits, pecans, candied ginger, lemon zest, and orange zest.
7. Pour the batter into the prepped loaf pan. Bake for 1 hour. Let the fruitcake cool in the pan.
8. In a small saucepan over medium heat, heat the apricot jam and rum for 2 to 3 minutes until glossy. Brush over the fruitcake.
9. Wrap the fruitcake in plastic wrap until ready to serve.
10. To make the icing: In a medium bowl, whisk together the confectioners sugar, milk, and lemon juice until smooth. Pour over the fruitcake.
11. To garnish: Decorate with cranberries, pecans, and rosemary. Sift the confectioners sugar on top before serving.

After those long days of showing tourists around the Clamp Centre, all I'd want was a big bowl of frozen yogurt. There's a nice yogurt stand in the building, but it's so popular. Those terrible, horrible stories about the gremlin that popped out of the candy topping tray haven't even put a dent into the wait since the building's been operational again! I decided that the only way to get my post-work frozen treat without having to stand in line for an hour or having to reminisce about those nasty creatures was to create my own recipe. –Kate

FROZEN YOGURT SURPRISE (GF, V)

PREP TIME: 30 minutes (plus 4 hours for freezing)
COOK TIME: N/A
YIELD: 2 servings
DIFFICULTY: Hard

INGREDIENTS

Pralines

¼ cup light brown sugar
1½ tablespoons heavy whipping cream
1 tablespoon salted butter
¼ cup confectioners sugar
½ teaspoon vanilla extract
¼ cup chopped pecans

Kona Yogurt

1½ cups plain Greek yogurt
¼ cup confectioners sugar
1 tablespoon espresso
1 teaspoon vanilla extract
¼ teaspoon kosher salt

Banana Berry Yogurt

1 cup frozen strawberries
½ cup sliced banana
½ cup plain Greek yogurt
1 tablespoon honey

Toppings

1 kiwi, peeled and sliced
½ cup mini peanut butter cups

DIRECTIONS

1. To make the pralines: Line a baking sheet with parchment paper.
2. In a medium saucepan over medium heat, bring the brown sugar, heavy whipping cream, and butter to a boil. Cook for 1 minute until the mixture starts to bubble.
3. Remove from heat, and whisk in the confectioners sugar and vanilla until the sugar has dissolved. Stir in the pecans.
4. Spread the mixture onto the prepped parchment paper. Let cool completely. Break into small pieces, and set aside.
5. To make the Kona yogurt: In a blender, add the Greek yogurt, confectioners sugar, espresso, vanilla, and salt until it's blended and fluffy. Pour into a sealable container, and freeze for 4 hours until scoopable.
6. To make the banana berry yogurt: In a blender add the frozen strawberries, banana, Greek yogurt, and honey. Blend until smooth. Pour into a sealable container, and freeze for 4 hours until scoopable.
7. Into a serving bowl, add one scoop of the banana berry yogurt. Add a scoop of the Kona yogurt, and top with pralines.
8. Top with kiwi and peanut butter cups, and serve.

I talked about these stupid jams seven times a day for months before I decided to try this promo recipe . . . and now it's the one thing I never want to forget about the Clamp Centre (but, boy, do I wish I could forget everything else . . .)! –Kate

Clamp's Jam Cookies (V)

You! You're an individual of vast insight and unquestionable taste! An honored visitor to the Clamp Premiere Regency Trade Centre and Retail Concourse, the most futuristic structure in New York! The Big Apple! The City That Never Sleeps! You've made the wise decision to purchase an assortment of Mr. Clamp's exceedingly popular jams and jellies, made from only the finest regionally sourced fruits! These jams and/ or jellies make an excellent spread for toast! Scones! Sandwiches! They're also excellent in baked goods! As our thanks to you, please accept this special bonus gift: the recipe for Mr. Clamp's favorite homemade cookies, just like Grandmother Clamp used to make!

PREP TIME: 1 hour 20 minutes
(plus 1 hour 20 minutes of refrigeration and cooling)
COOK TIME: 14 minutes
YIELD: 32 cookies
DIFFICULTY: Easy

INGREDIENTS

1 cup (2 sticks) unsalted butter, softened
⅔ cup granulated sugar
2 large egg yolks
½ teaspoon almond extract
½ teaspoon vanilla extract
2½ cups all-purpose flour
¼ teaspoon kosher salt
⅓ cup strawberry jam
⅓ cup apricot jam

DIRECTIONS

1. Prep a baking sheet with parchment paper. Set aside.
2. In the bowl of an electric mixer, cream together the butter and sugar for 1 to 2 minutes until fluffy.
3. Stir in the egg yolks, almond extract, and vanilla.
4. Add the flour and salt until just combined.
5. Roll the dough into tablespoon-size balls, and place them onto the prepped baking sheet 2 inches apart.
6. Press the back of a teaspoon into the center of each ball to create an indentation. Fill each cookie with strawberry or apricot jam. Refrigerate for 1 hour.
7. Preheat the oven to 350°F. Bake for 14 minutes until lightly golden.
8. Let the cookies cool on the pan for 20 minutes; then move them to a wire rack to cool completely.

GREMLIN S'MORES (V)

A few things in life should never be argued about. First, when it comes to mogwai, it always pays to follow the rules. Second, comics should be held in higher esteem, as one of the few original artforms created by Americans. And third, the best s'mores have marshmallows with a bubbling, blackened crust. I lost my taste for charred marshmallows for a little while after seeing a theater full of gremlins melted into goo by a fire, but they won me back. —*Billy*

PREP TIME: 15 minutes (plus 1 hour of refrigeration)
COOK TIME: 12 minutes
YIELD: 12 servings
DIFFICULTY: Moderate

INGREDIENTS

Graham Crackers
1½ cups whole-wheat flour
½ cup all-purpose flour
1 tablespoon matcha powder
½ teaspoon cinnamon
½ teaspoon baking soda
¼ teaspoon kosher salt
¼ teaspoon ground nutmeg
½ cup (1 stick) unsalted butter, softened
½ cup packed light brown sugar
⅓ cup honey
1½ teaspoons vanilla extract
¼ cup whole milk

S'mores
Six 1.5-ounce chocolate bars
10 ounces mini marshmallows
1 tablespoon matcha powder

DIRECTIONS

1. To make the graham crackers: In a medium bowl, whisk together the whole-wheat flour, all-purpose flour, matcha powder, cinnamon, baking soda, salt, and nutmeg.
2. In the bowl of an electric mixer, cream together the butter, brown sugar, honey, and vanilla for 2 minutes until fluffy.
3. Add the dry ingredients and milk, and mix just until the dough comes together.
4. Roll out the dough between two sheets of parchment paper to 1/16 inch. Refrigerate for 1 hour.
5. Preheat the oven to 350°F. Line a baking sheet with parchment paper.
6. Cut the dough into 4-inch squares. Transfer to the prepped baking sheet.
7. Bake for 12 minutes until the edges are lightly browned. Let the graham crackers cool on a wire rack.
8. To make the s'mores: Place 12 graham crackers onto a baking sheet. Top with a piece of chocolate and ¼ cup mini marshmallows.
9. Use a kitchen torch to toast the marshmallows and melt the chocolate. Top with the remaining 12 graham crackers.
10. Dust with matcha powder, and serve.

BAVARIAN SNOW CONES (V)

Even though gremlins are little chaos monsters, they weren't even close to the most terrifying thing Kingston Falls had ever seen—that was Mrs. Deagle. With gremlins, if you followed all the rules, you could be safe. With Mrs. Deagle, you couldn't ever be sure. Once, after our dog, Barney, accidentally knocked over a Bavarian snowman decoration in her yard, Mrs. Deagle tried to have him taken away. Who does that? Especially at Christmas? Mrs. Deagle, that's who. I think I have more nightmares about that woman than I do any gremlin—and these snow cones look like the snowman she claimed Barney broke. Gosh, if I'm lucky, maybe eating these will scare her memory away, too! —*Billy*

PREP TIME: 10 minutes (plus 24 hours for freezing)
COOK TIME: N/A
YIELD: 2 servings
DIFFICULTY: Easy

INGREDIENTS

Ice
2 cups coconut milk
14 ounces sweetened condensed milk

Decorations
4 chocolate chips
2 small pieces of orange fondant
4 pretzel sticks
2 sour strip candies

DIRECTIONS

1. To make the ice: In a large bowl, whisk together the coconut milk and sweetened condensed milk. Pour into ice cube trays, and freeze overnight.
2. Use a blender or an ice shaver to shave the ice cubes into fluffy ice. Scoop a large scoop into two bowls, and then add a smaller scoop on top.
3. To decorate: Use the chocolate chips for eyes, orange fondant for the nose, and pretzel sticks for the arms.
4. Finish with a candy strip scarf, and serve.

SMASHED APPLE PIES (V)

Sometimes I think that maybe bad luck follows me wherever I go. I mean, two separate times in my life already, an army of three-foot-tall monsters has tried to kill me. (I hope no one reading this has said, "Third time's the charm.") But the gremlin experience has at least taught me one thing: how to get past adversity. Case in point: Not long ago, my mother sent a homemade apple pie all the way from Pennsylvania—by bus! I love my mom's homemade apple pie almost as much as I love drawing. I was dreaming about it. When it finally got here and was put in my hands, I found out that it had been sat on and crushed! But you know what? There's nothing wrong with a smashed apple pie. I might even like it better that way. —Billy

PREP TIME: 10 minutes
COOK TIME: 20 minutes
YIELD: 8 servings
DIFFICULTY: Easy

INGREDIENTS

¾ cup honey
2 large Granny Smith apples, cored and thinly sliced
⅓ cup light brown sugar
2 teaspoons cinnamon
1 teaspoon ground nutmeg
½ teaspoon kosher salt
2 sheets puff pastry, thawed
1 egg, beaten, plus 1 tablespoon water, for egg wash
2 tablespoons confectioners sugar, for dusting

DIRECTIONS

1. Preheat the oven to 400°F. Line two baking sheets with parchment paper.
2. Drizzle the honey onto each of the four quadrants of both baking sheets.
3. Top with the sliced apples.
4. Sprinkle with brown sugar, cinnamon, nutmeg, and salt.
5. Cut the puff pastry into 8 equal squares. Place one square over the apples in one of the quadrants, securing the edges.
6. Brush with egg wash. Repeat with the remaining pastry squares and apples.
7. Bake for 20 minutes. Turn each pastry square over, and let cool apple side up on a wire rack.
8. Dust with confectioners sugar, and serve.

CHOCOLATE MOUSSE (GF,V)

Like I've said many times now, I never got any dessert during my completely innocent work dinner, but I do love a good chocolate mousse. The Canadian restaurant's version was more a block of moose-shape chocolate than a chocolate mousse. I've gotta say, they really do stay on brand over there. All things considered, I'm just happy I got out of that place without a gremlin in a Mountie uniform chasing me with an electric carving knife or a chainsaw or something. *—Billy*

PREP TIME: 20 minutes (plus 1 hour of refrigeration)
COOK TIME: 4 minutes
YIELD: 6 servings
DIFFICULTY: Easy

INGREDIENTS

4 large egg yolks
2 tablespoons granulated sugar
1 cup half and half
4 ounces dark chocolate, chopped
4 ounces semisweet chocolate, chopped
1 teaspoon vanilla extract
¼ teaspoon kosher salt
1 cup heavy whipping cream
2 tablespoons confectioners sugar
1 cup whipped cream, for serving
1 tablespoon cocoa powder, for dusting

DIRECTIONS

1. Over a double boiler, whisk together the egg yolks, sugar, and half and half. Cook for 3 to 4 minutes until slightly thickened.
2. Stir in the dark chocolate and semisweet chocolate until melted.
3. Remove from heat. Whisk in the vanilla and salt.
4. Set aside in the refrigerator to cool for 1 hour.
5. In a large bowl with a hand mixer, beat together the heavy whipping cream and confectioners sugar until stiff peaks form.
6. Fold the whipping cream mixture into the cooled chocolate mixture until combined.
7. Spoon into serving dishes, and refrigerate.
8. When ready to serve, garnish with whipped cream and dust with cocoa powder.

NEW YORK CHEESECAKE (GF, V)

It's important to note that gremlins love to have a good time. In fact, they're happiest when they can sing and party while simultaneously hurting someone or breaking something. The good news is that this makes a gremlin very easy to distract—and that can make all the difference. I don't know if we could've kept the Clamp Centre infestation from escaping into New York City if the gremlins hadn't decided to break into a rousing version of "New York, New York." I'm still trying to figure out exactly how they knew the words to the song in the first place. Maybe they were inspired by a really good piece of cheesecake? —Billy

PREP TIME: 25 minutes (plus 24 hours for refrigeration)
COOK TIME: 1 hour 42 minutes
YIELD: 8 servings
DIFFICULTY: Hard

INGREDIENTS

Crust

1½ cups Killer Gingerbread Cookies crumbs (page 76)
6 tablespoons unsalted butter, melted
2 tablespoons light brown sugar
¼ teaspoon kosher salt

Filling

32 ounces cream cheese, softened
1¾ cups granulated sugar
3 tablespoons cornstarch
1 tablespoon lemon juice
1 tablespoon vanilla extract
¼ teaspoon kosher salt
6 large eggs, room temperature
½ cup sour cream

Strawberry Topping

2 quarts strawberries, diced
⅔ cup granulated sugar
1 tablespoon lemon juice

DIRECTIONS

1. Preheat the oven to 350°F. Wrap a 10-inch springform pan with heavy-duty aluminum foil.
2. To make the crust: In a medium bowl, stir together the cookie crumbs, butter, brown sugar and salt, until combined. Press the mixture into the bottom of the prepped pan. Bake the crust for 10 to 12 minutes until lightly browned. Let cool completely.
3. Reduce the oven temperature to 300°F.
4. To make the filling: In the bowl of an electric mixer on medium speed, beat together the cream cheese, sugar, cornstarch, lemon juice, vanilla, and salt until just combined.
5. Reduce the speed to low, and add the eggs one at a time. Stir in the sour cream, and mix until just combined but the batter is smooth.
6. Place the wrapped springform pan in a large roasting pan. Pour the batter on top of the crust.
7. Make a water bath by pouring boiling water into the roasting pan up to 1 inch on the side of the springform pan. Bake for 1½ hours until the cake is just set and slightly wobbly.
8. Remove the roasting pan from the oven, leaving the cheesecake in the water bath and untouched for 2 hours.
9. Remove the springform pan from the water bath, and run a knife around the edge of the cake to loosen it from the edge. Discard the foil. Cover the pan with plastic wrap, and place it in the refrigerator to cool overnight.
10. To make the strawberry topping: Set aside half of the strawberries. Place the other half into a medium saucepan, and add the sugar. Over medium-low heat, bring to a low simmer until the strawberries have slightly macerated. Lightly crush the strawberries with a masher.
11. Pour into a medium bowl, and stir in the reserved strawberries. Set aside to cool or refrigerate until ready to serve.
12. Release the springform pan, removing the ring.
13. Spoon the strawberry topping over the cheesecake. Slice, and then serve.

Drinks

Remember, man might be able to live on water alone, but there's no sense in doing so when there are many other fun beverages to wet your whistle. When you can sit down with drinks for morning, noon, and night, it'll take your palate a while to get bored, believe you me—and don't forget that there's a Peltzer product for everything potable. (You might not need them, but keep that information to yourself, and send all curious parties my way for coffee makers, aerators, and more!) - RAND

BLENDED GREMLIN SMOOTHIE (GF, V, V+)

This smoothie looks like what happened to one of the little green beasts that destroyed my kitchen after it made the mistake of getting caught in a blender. Whenever I make this, I get to remember that I was able to beat the gremlins back myself, and that is a powerful feeling, Billy! But that is not the main reason I like this recipe. Mostly, it is because I enjoy a nice, healthy smoothie every now and again. I find them so refreshing! (I cannot say that your father agrees with me, but at least he is drinking more juice these days.) –Lynn

PREP TIME: 5 minutes
COOK TIME: N/A
YIELD: 1 serving
DIFFICULTY: Easy

INGREDIENTS

2 cups fresh baby spinach, plus 2 leaves for garnish
1 cup frozen pineapple
½ cup diced green apple
1 cup coconut water

DIRECTIONS

1. In a blender, add the spinach, pineapple, green apple, and coconut water. Blend until smooth.
2. Pour into a tall glass. Garnish with spinach leaves.

SHERIFF FRANK'S EGGNOG (GF, V)

You know, eggnog is everywhere during the holiday season, but it is gone from the stores before the new year. Like clockwork, I get a craving for a cup right around springtime. I mentioned this once, and Sheriff Frank replied that he had the same problem—but he also had the perfect recipe for homemade eggnog. Can you believe it? I admit, Frank never struck me as the type of person who would know the first thing about being in the kitchen. (You would think, after seeing what happens to a mogwai, that I would have learned to not judge a book by its cover.) Gentle life lesson aside, this eggnog is delicious. Try some! —Lynn

PREP TIME: 20 minutes
COOK TIME: 10 minutes
YIELD: 4 servings
DIFFICULTY: Moderate

INGREDIENTS

2 cups whole milk
1 cinnamon stick
1 star anise
1 tablespoon whole cloves
5 large egg yolks
1 cup granulated sugar
1½ teaspoons vanilla extract
1½ cups half and half
Whipped cream, for serving
1 tablespoon granulated sugar, for garnish
½ teaspoon cinnamon, for garnish

DIRECTIONS

1. In a large saucepan over medium-high heat, add the milk, cinnamon stick, star anise, and cloves. Bring to a low simmer; then remove from heat, and set aside.
2. In a large bowl, whisk together the egg yolks, sugar, and vanilla. Temper the eggs by slowly whisking in the hot milk mixture a ladle at a time until fully incorporated.
3. Pour the milk back into the saucepan. Over medium-low heat, simmer while whisking for 2 to 3 minutes or until just thickened.
4. Strain the eggnog, to discard the cinnamon stick, star anise, and cloves.
5. Stir in the half and half. Pour the liquid into a pitcher, and refrigerate overnight.
6. Pour the eggnog into serving glasses. Top with whipped cream, sprinkle with sugar and cinnamon, and serve.

KINGSTON FALLS HOLIDAY COCOA (V)

Sheriff Frank's eggnog recipe got me thinking about other Christmas drinks. My absolute favorite, besides eggnog, was the hot cocoa at the lot downtown where Pete's family sold Christmas trees. I used to tell your father that they kept some families from buying an artificial tree just to keep getting that cocoa every year. In fact, I bet they could have made just as much money, if not more, if they had opened a concession stand and sold the cocoa to the locals instead of selling Christmas trees! You are an artist, sweetheart, so you know that presentation is important. Do not forget to include a candy cane when you have a cup! —Lynn

PREP TIME: 5 minutes
COOK TIME: 5 minutes
YIELD: 2 servings
DIFFICULTY: Easy

INGREDIENTS

Whipped Cream

2 ounces mascarpone cheese, softened
¼ cup confectioners sugar
½ teaspoon vanilla extract
¼ teaspoon kosher salt
½ cup heavy whipping cream

Cocoa

1 cup whole milk
1 cup half and half
½ cup chopped dark chocolate
1 teaspoon vanilla extract

Garnish

¼ cup crushed Killer Gingerbread Cookies (page 76)
2 rosemary sprigs
2 mini candy canes

DIRECTIONS

1. To make the whipped cream: In a medium bowl, use a hand mixer to stir together the mascarpone, confectioners sugar, vanilla, and salt. Add the heavy whipping cream, and whip until light and fluffy, about 1 to 2 minutes. Keep in the refrigerator to chill.
2. To make the cocoa: In a saucepan over medium-low heat, add the milk, half and half, dark chocolate, and vanilla.
3. Whisk, and bring to a low simmer. Cook for 2 minutes until smooth.
4. Pour into two mugs. Top with the whipped cream.
5. To garnish: Sprinkle the crushed gingerbread cookies on top, and add the rosemary and mini candy canes.

Sunkist
Juicer

PELTZER'S PERFECT MOCHA (GF, V)

Follow me on this, son. You're working your tail off at your 9-to-5, nose to the grindstone. Suddenly, you're out of juice. You want a nap, but you're at work–you can't just go to sleep. And the coffee from the machine in the office is so weak that it couldn't keep a kitten awake. What do you do? You reach into your thermos for a sip of Peltzer's Perfect Mocha. That's right, it's all the caffeine you need to put the pep back into your step, and it's made effortlessly with the Peltzer Coffee Maker. But say you're the type of person who doesn't have a Peltzer Coffee Maker handy. Not a problem–just follow this simple recipe, and you'll have yourself a cup of pure energy before you know it. (But I do recommend the coffee maker.)

- RAND

PREP TIME: 10 minutes
COOK TIME: 1 minute
YIELD: 1 serving
DIFFICULTY: Easy

INGREDIENTS

Whipped Cream

½ cup heavy whipping cream, chilled
1 tablespoon confectioners sugar
½ teaspoon vanilla extract

Mocha

1 cup whole milk
1 ounce dark chocolate
2 ounces espresso
1 tablespoon chocolate syrup, for garnish

DIRECTIONS

1. To make the whipped cream: In a chilled bowl with a hand mixer, whip the heavy cream, confectioners sugar, and vanilla until soft peaks form. Refrigerate until ready to use.
2. To make the mocha: Pour the milk into a medium mason jar. Tighten the lid, and shake for 20 to 30 seconds until frothy.
3. Remove the lid, and microwave the milk for 45 to 60 seconds until hot.
4. Add the dark chocolate to a large coffee mug. Pour in the espresso and then the steamed milk.
5. Top with whipped cream, drizzle with chocolate syrup, and serve.

ORANGE JUICE SPRITZ (GF, V, V+)

To my mind, most days of the week, there's nothing better first thing in the morning than a fresh-brewed cup of joe. But some days, you're just not in the mood. You need another kind of a pick-me-up, and a glass of all-American orange juice is the perfect choice. Used to be that your only choice was to have it with pulp or without . . . but thanks to a quirk of the Peltzer Peeler-Juicer, I've found another way to enjoy OJ: with fizz! (Aerated is the technical term, but you won't impress anyone with that.) This preparation could change breakfast as we know it, and you can even make it without the Peltzer Peeler-Juicer (but don't tell anybody that—have them send for my catalog). - RAND

PREP TIME: 20 minutes
COOK TIME: 3 minutes
YIELD: 4 servings
DIFFICULTY: Easy

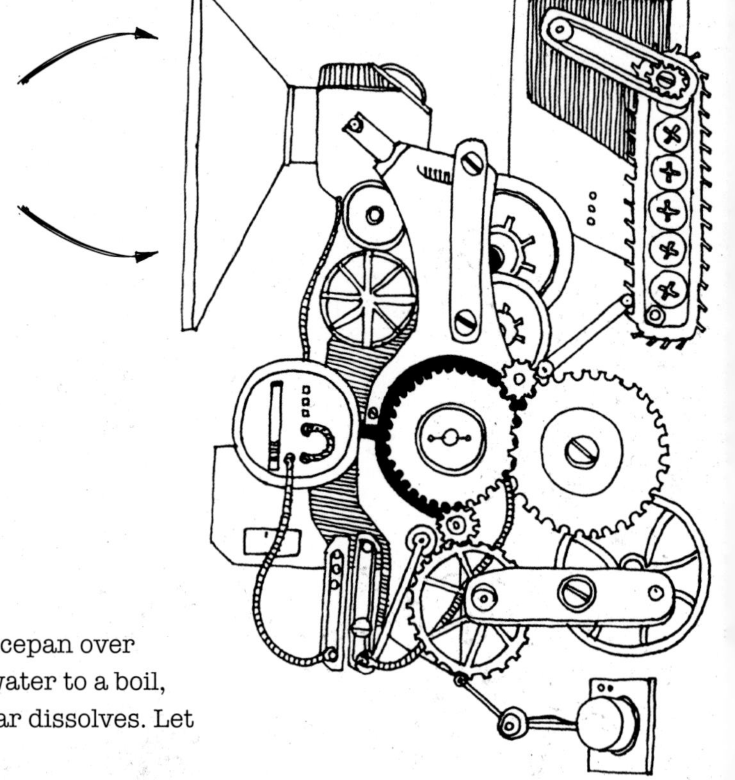

INGREDIENTS

Simple Syrup

1 cup granulated sugar
1 cup water

Juice

9 large oranges
2 tablespoons fresh lemon juice
3 cups sparkling water, cold

DIRECTIONS

1. To make the simple syrup: In a small saucepan over medium-high heat, bring the sugar and water to a boil, and cook for 2 to 3 minutes until the sugar dissolves. Let cool completely.
2. To make the juice: Juice the oranges. Strain with a sieve, and discard the pulp.
3. In a large pitcher, stir together the orange juice, lemon juice, and cooled simple syrup. Stir in the sparkling water.
4. Pour into glasses filled with ice, and serve.

MR. WING'S MILK TEA (GF, V, V+)

Every time I get a chance to visit Chinatown, I come away with an appreciation for new food. Had my first glass of this refreshing milk tea on the recommendation of old Mr. Wing last time I was in his neck of the woods. (I think he might've been trying to get out of my pitching him on an automated teapot.) Funny thing about this tea—and maybe it's why he likes it—it's kind of colored like our little friend, Gizmo. – RAND

PREP TIME: 10 minutes (plus 55 minutes for soaking)
COOK TIME: 28 minutes
YIELD: 1 serving
DIFFICULTY: Moderate

INGREDIENTS

Boba Simple Syrup
1 cup water
1 cup light brown sugar
¼ teaspoon vanilla extract

Boba
5 cups water
¼ cup boba pearls

Matcha
¾ cup hot water
1 teaspoon matcha powder

Milk
½ cup coconut milk
1 tablespoon confectioners sugar

DIRECTIONS

1. To make the simple syrup: In a small saucepan over high heat, combine 1 cup water and brown sugar. Boil for 2 to 3 minutes until the sugars have dissolved. Let cool; then stir in the vanilla, and set aside.
2. To make the boba: In a large saucepan over medium-high heat, bring 5 cups of water to a boil. Add the boba, turn down the heat, and simmer for 25 minutes. Turn off the heat, cover the saucepan, and let the boba sit for another 25 minutes.
3. Drain and rinse the boba, and then pour it into the cooled simple syrup. Let soak for 30 minutes.
4. To make the matcha: In a mason jar, add the water and matcha. Shake vigorously for 15 to 20 seconds until the matcha has dissolved. Set aside.
5. To make the milk: In a small bowl, whisk together the coconut milk and confectioners sugar until the sugar has dissolved.
6. To assemble, scoop the boba into a tall glass. Add ice.
7. Pour in first the coconut milk and then pour the matcha mixture, and serve.

DORRY'S TAVERN SPECIAL (GF, V)

One of the things that I love the most about Kingston Falls is Dorry's Tavern. Dorry's wasn't just the kind of place where everybody's dad proposed to their mom. It's one of those special places with the kind of charm you can only ever find in a small town. I'm glad we got the town to sign the petition to save the tavern, but sometimes when I think about that special place, I'm taken back to that one night—that dark, snowy night and those crazy, terrible creatures. Thank god Dorry was able to repair the damage after those horrible gremlins wreaked havoc! In any case, this cola float with popping candy reminds me of home and Dorry's Tavern every time I make it. And it's a nice reminder that it's important to hold the good memories closer than the bad ones . . . . –Kate

PREP TIME: 10 minutes
COOK TIME: N/A
YIELD: 1 serving
DIFFICULTY: Easy

INGREDIENTS

1 ounce grenadine
2 teaspoons vanilla syrup
12 ounces cola
1 cup (2 scoops) vanilla ice cream
¼ cup whipped cream
3 tablespoons green popping candy
1 maraschino cherry

DIRECTIONS

1. In a tall glass, combine the grenadine and vanilla syrup. Pour in the cola, and add the ice cream.
2. Top with whipped cream, sprinkle with popping candy, and place the cherry atop the whipped cream; then serve.

BUBBLY POOL PUNCH (GF, V)

An important rule for mogwai care is to never let them get wet. If they do get wet, there's an immediate reaction, and suddenly you have more mogwai than you started with. The scary part is that the same rule is true for gremlins—and I saw it firsthand. I was chasing Stripe, the alpha gremlin, trying to catch him before he could hurt anybody else. Stripe ran into the YMCA, looking for a good hiding place, and instead he found an Olympic-size swimming pool. Gosh, this punch looks a lot like the aftermath of a gremlin taking a swim, so it's great reminder for rule number 2. —*Billy*

PREP TIME: 10 minutes
COOK TIME: N/A
YIELD: 10 servings
DIFFICULTY: Easy

INGREDIENTS

One 6-ounce package lime gelatin
2 cups boiling water
4 cups pineapple juice
4 cups limeade
2 liters lemon-lime soda
½ gallon vanilla ice cream
Lime wheels, to garnish

DIRECTIONS

1. Dissolve the gelatin in the water.
2. Pour the gelatin/water mixture into a large punch bowl. Stir in the pineapple juice, limeade, and lemon-lime soda.
3. Add scoops of vanilla ice cream, and serve in glasses garnished with lime wheels.

BRIGHT LIGHT TEA (GF, V, V+)

Mogwai, and the rules about caring for them, should be better known by people. This would've come in handy for an assignment I'd had in the art department for an easy-to-make "Clamp's Mix" of tea and lemonade. The idea for the campaign was that the drink made you feel as bright and shiny as the morning sun. All I could think about was mogwai rule number one: Bright light, especially sunlight, will kill a mogwai—or a gremlin. Can you imagine that as a commercial? I bet it would've won an award—well, maybe at a horror convention. Either way, this tea is a great reminder for rule number 1. —*Billy*

PREP TIME: 10 minutes (plus 2½ hours for steeping)
COOK TIME: N/A
YIELD: 8 servings
DIFFICULTY: Moderate

INGREDIENTS

Tea
8 cups water
6 black tea bags

Simple Syrup
2 cups water
1½ cups granulated sugar

Lemonade
9 large lemons, juiced (equal to 1½ cups juice)
6 cups cold water
Lemon slices, for garnish

DIRECTIONS

1. To make the tea: Place the water and tea bags into a large clear jar. Close the lid, and place the jar in direct sunlight. Let steep for 2½ hours. Remove the tea bags, and refrigerate the liquid until ready to use.
2. To make the simple syrup: In a large saucepan over medium heat, bring the water and sugar to a boil, and cook until the sugar dissolves. Remove from heat, and let cool completely.
3. To make the lemonade: In a large pitcher, stir together the lemon juice, cold water, and simple syrup.
4. Fill tall glasses with ice. Pour in 1 cup of lemonade, top with 1 cup of tea, and garnish with lemon slices.

SPLICE

MOHAWK MUDSLIDE (V)

I think there should be a fourth rule for mogwai: Don't get them wet, keep them away from bright light, don't feed them after midnight, and if you spot any that have a mohawk, get away from them as fast as you can—they're going to be extra dangerous. I guess maybe I shouldn't assume such a thing, but when have there been two in a row? That feels like a pattern to me, so keep that in mind. It was so bad that now I'm nervous any time I even see a mohawk, which can make riding the subway a problem. —*Billy*

PREP TIME: 10 minutes
COOK TIME: N/A
YIELD: 1 serving
DIFFICULTY: Easy

INGREDIENTS

1 pint vanilla ice cream
1 cup whole milk
3 tablespoons chocolate syrup
1 teaspoon espresso powder
½ teaspoon vanilla extract
1 cup whipped cream, divided
4 chocolate sandwich cookies, crushed

DIRECTIONS

1. In a blender, add the ice cream, milk, chocolate syrup, espresso powder, and vanilla. Blend until smooth.
2. Pour half the mixture into a tall glass. Top with ½ cup whipped cream and half of the crushed cookies.
3. Pour the rest of the blended mixture into the glass, and top with the remaining cookies.
4. With the remaining whipped cream, create a mohawk on top; then serve.

DIETARY CONSIDERATION CHART

Gremlin Fingers	GF, V, V+
Gremlin Wings	GF
Homemade Fruit Leather	GF, V
Microwave Popcorn	GF, V
Mr. Hanson's Candy Bar Salad	V
Chinatown Wonton Soup	
Daffy's Corn on the Cob	GF, V
Jellied Gremlin Guts	GF, V
Hatching Cocoons	GF
Rockin' Ricky Rialto Whipped Feta	GF, V
Mogwai Puffs	V
Excessive Onion Dip	GF, V
Artichoke-Powered Appetizer	GF, V
Greta's Midnight Kisses	V
Grandpa Fred's Octopus Appetizer	
High-Voltage Cheese	V
Vegetable Medley	GF, V, V+
Healing Chicken Soup	
Roasted Gremlin Chops	GF
Christmas Ham	GF
Five-Egg Omelet	GF, V
Kate's Comfort PB&J	V
Secretary's Snappy Sandwich	V
Tuna Noodle Cheese Product Chowder Surprise	
Don't Get It Wet Burrito	

Midnight Fried Chicken	
Murray's Meatloaf	
Canadian Cleaned Fish	
Clamp's Shredded Salad	GF
Gremlin Scones	V
Killer Gingerbread Cookies	V
Midnight Snack Cakes	V
Kate's Hated Holiday Fruitcake	V
Frozen Yogurt Surprise	GF, V
Clamp's Jam Cookies	V
Gremlin S'mores	V
Bavarian Snow Cones	V
Smashed Apple Pies	V
Chocolate Mousse	GF, V
New York Cheesecake	V
Blended Gremlin Smoothie	GF, V, V+
Sheriff Frank's Eggnog	GF, V
Kingston Falls Holiday Cocoa	V
Peltzer's Perfect Mocha	GF, V
Orange Juice Spritz	GF, V, V+
Mr. Wing's Milk Tea	GF, V, V+
Dorry's Tavern Special	GF, V
Bubbly Pool Punch	GF, V
Bright Light Tea	GF, V, V+
Mohawk Mudslide	V

METRIC CONVERSION CHART

KITCHEN MEASUREMENTS

Cups	Tablespoons	Teaspoons	Fluid Ounces
1/16 cup	1 tablespoon	3 teaspoons	½ fluid ounce
⅛ cup	2 tablespoons	6 teaspoons	1 fluid ounce
¼ cup	4 tablespoons	12 teaspoons	2 fluid ounces
⅓ cup	5½ tablespoons	16 teaspoons	2⅔ fluid ounces
½ cup	8 tablespoons	24 teaspoons	4 fluid ounces
⅔ cup	10⅔ tablespoons	32 teaspoons	5⅓ fluid ounces
¾ cup	12 tablespoons	36 teaspoons	6 fluid ounces
1 cup	16 tablespoons	48 teaspoons	8 fluid ounces

Gallons	Quarts	Pints	Cups	Fluid Ounces
1/16 gallon	¼ quart	½ pint	1 cup	8 fluid ounces
⅛ gallon	½ quart	1 pint	2 cups	16 fluid ounces
¼ gallon	1 quart	2 pints	4 cups	32 fluid ounces
½ gallon	2 quarts	4 pints	8 cups	64 fluid ounces
1 gallon	4 quarts	8 pints	16 cups	128 fluid ounces

LENGTH

Imperial	Metric
1 inch	2.5 centimeters
2 inches	5 centimeters
4 inches	10 centimeters
6 inches	15 centimeters
8 inches	20 centimeters
10 inches	25 centimeters

WEIGHT

Grams	Ounces
14 grams	½ ounce
28 grams	1 ounce
57 grams	2 ounces
85 grams	3 ounces
113 grams	4 ounces
142 grams	5 ounces
170 grams	6 ounces
283 grams	10 ounces
397 grams	14 ounces
454 grams	16 ounces
907 grams	32 ounces

OVEN TEMPERATURES

Fahrenheit	Celsius
200°F	93°C
225°F	107°C
250°F	121°C
275°F	135°C
300°F	149°C
325°F	163°C
350°F	177°C
375°F	191°C
400°F	204°C
425°F	218°C
450°F	232°C

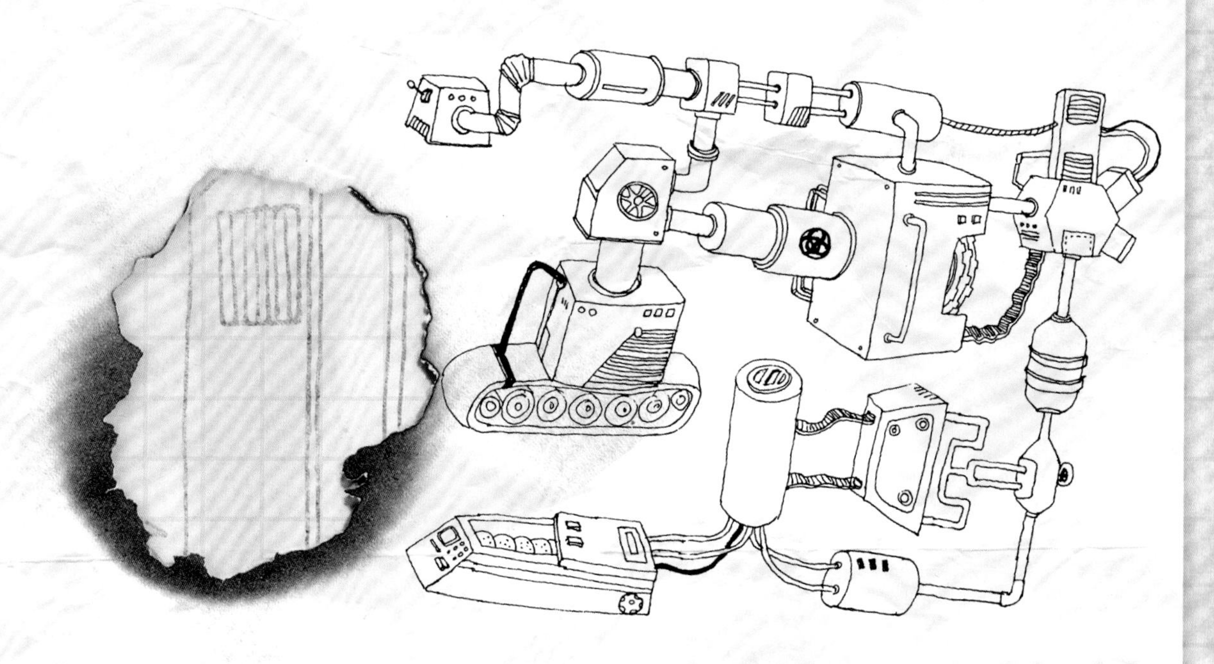

FRY STATION SAFETY TIPS

If you're making something that requires deep frying, here are some important tips to prevent any kitchen fires:

1. If you don't have a dedicated deep fryer, use a Dutch oven or a high-walled sauté pan.
2. Never use too much oil in the pan! You don't want hot oil spilling out as soon as you put the food in.
3. Use only a suitable cooking oil, like canola, peanut, or vegetable oil.
4. Always keep track of the oil temperature with a thermometer—350°F to 375°F should do the trick.
5. Never put too much food in the pan at the same time!
6. Never put wet food in the pan; it will splatter and may cause burns.
7. Always have a lid nearby to cover the pan, in case it starts to spill over or catch fire. A properly rated fire extinguisher is also great to have on hand in case of emergencies.
8. Never leave the pan unattended, and never let children near the pan.
9. Never, ever put your face, hand, or any other body part in the hot oil.

MOGWAI SAFETY TIPS

There's three important rules you've gotta follow:

Number one, mogwais hate bright lights. You gotta keep them out of the sunlight—sunlight will kill 'em.

Number two, keep mogwai away from water. Don't give them any water to drink, and whatever you do, don't give 'em a bath.

And the most important rule—the rule you can never forget—no matter how much he cries or how much he begs, never, never feed 'em after midnight. —Billy

GLOSSARY

COOKING TERMS

BASTE: When a recipe calls for basting, it means to pour, spoon, or brush liquid over food, most often meat or poultry, to give it good flavor and color during roasting.

DREDGE: To coat with flour or another dry ingredient, such as cornmeal or bread crumbs, often seasoned. Food is sprinkled with the dry ingredient, dragged through it, or shaken with it. Alternatively, the food and coating may be placed in a plastic bag and shaken together. After dredging, the food should be shaken to remove excess coating. Do not dredge food too far in advance of cooking, or the coating will absorb moisture from the food and become gummy. Laying dredged food on a wire rack also helps avoid gumminess. Dredged food is usually sauteed, fried or deep-fried, or baked. The coating helps it brown nicely and retain moisture, and adds a nice crispiness.

JULIENNE: Refers to cutting food into long, thin strips, which in turn are called a "julienne."

KNEAD: Uncover the dough and knead it by using the heel of one hand to push the dough away from you and then pull it back with your fingertips. Turn and repeat until the dough is smooth and elastic, 5 to 7 minutes.

MINCE: Gather the leaves together and rock the blade over them until they are chopped into small, even pieces (finely chopped), or into pieces as fine as possible (minced).

ROAST: Roasting meats and poultry in an uncovered roasting pan in a hot oven intensifies their flavors. Because the oven does most of the work, this technique requires little hands-on cooking time. Before you start, line a heavy roasting pan with aluminum foil and brush the foil with a little olive oil to help prevent sticking.

SIFT: The process of putting flour, confectioners sugar, or cornstarch through a fine-mesh sieve to aerate and remove lumps. Multiple ingredients—such as flour, salt, and leavenings—are often sifted together to blend them.

SIMMER: Simmering calls for consistent, medium-to-small bubbles . . .Simmering and poaching are moist-heat cooking techniques that gently cook foods to tenderness in a hot liquid . . .You don't need special cookware for simmering. Any saucepan or sauté pan will do, although if you intend to reduce a volume of liquid, a pan with a wide base and large surface area will help the process go faster.

COOKING UTENSILS

BAKING DISH: Shallow, rectangular dishes made of tempered glass, porcelain, or earthenware are all-purpose vessels that work for roasting meat or vegetables and baking brownies or bread pudding. Items will cook more slowly in opaque ceramic than they will in clear glass.

BAKING PAN: Use these pans, which typically measure 9-by-13 inches with sides 2 to 2½ inches high, for baking sheet cakes, brownies, corn bread and coffee cakes. You can also use these pans for making casseroles.

BAKING SHEET: A baking sheet (also called a sheet pan) is a rectangular metal pan with shallow, slightly sloping rims. Choose sturdy stainless-steel ones that will last for years.

DUTCH OVEN: A large heavy cooking pot usually made of cast iron. This can go on the stove or in the oven and is great at retaining heat, making it the perfect cooking vessel for just about everything.

HIGH-HEAT VS. NONSTICK PANS: A high-heat pan—as its name suggests—can stand up to high-heat cooking, generally temperatures between 400°F and 600°F. They're usually made of stainless steel, cast iron, or enameled cast iron and can be used on the stovetop or oven—if the handle is made of an ovenproof material. Nonstick cookware contains a coating that helps keeps foods from sticking (particularly eggs), but they can't be used at the same temperatures as high-heat pans. If you are cooking with nonstick cookware, make sure you know the manufacturer's heat limits for your cookware. Most nonstick cookware should not be used at above medium heat on a stovetop (about 350°F) and is not generally suitable for the oven.

SAUCEPAN: This simple round pan has either straight or slightly sloping sides and generally ranges in size from 1 to 5 quarts. If you are buying only one, consider a 2-quart saucepan, which is most versatile. The pans are designed to facilitate rapid evaporation so that a sauce thickens and cooks efficiently. Straight-sided pans with high sides are ideal for longer cooking, since the liquid will not evaporate as quickly.

SAUTÉ PAN: Sauté pans have high, angled handles and relatively high sides to help prevent food from bouncing out of the pan when it is being stirred, turned, or flipped. The sides can range from 2½ to 4 inches high, with 3 inches being the most popular. Sauté pans can measure from 6 to 14¼ inches in diameter, and volume capacities generally range from 1 to 7 quarts, with 2½ to 4 quarts being the most useful for home cooks. Sauté pans often come with lids, which are useful for containing evaporation in recipes that call for long, gentle simmering. For this reason, sauté pans are also nicely suited to braises or any stove top recipes that call for large amounts of liquid.

ABOUT THE AUTHORS

Jenn Fujikawa is a lifestyle and pop culture author, content creator, and host. She has created content for Lucasfilm, Marvel, Disney, and more. Jenn is the author of multiple fandom-based cookbooks including *Star Wars: The Life Day Cookbook*, *Star Wars: The Padawan Cookbook*, *Ghostbusters:*
The Official Cookbook, *Parks and Recreation: The Official Cookbook*, *The Princess Bride: The Official Cookbook*, and many more. For more of her recipes check out her Instagram, @justjennrecipes.

ERIK BURNHAM was convinced that he should be a magician, but with no manual dexterity he instead gravitated to creating stories. He is best known for writing comic books of beloved franchises such as Ghostbusters, Back to the Future, and Teenage Mutant Ninja Turtles. He calls Minnesota home—and you betcha, it's chilly there. You can find him online at www.burnhamania.com, or on social media @erikburnham.

ACKNOWLEDGMENTS

From Jenn

Thank you to my family who encourage the Peltzer-like inventiveness in me: Alice Kawakami; Kyle, Tyler, and Mason Fujikawa; and Mark Kawakami. To Becky and Joel Okada who enjoyed the Candy Bar Salad. To the crew who would fight off Gremlins by my side: AJ Camarillo, Mel Caylo, Cheryl deCarvalho, Chrissy Dinh, Chrys Hasegawa, Sarah Kuhn, and Robb Pearlman. To Erik Burnham, my partner in all things 80s. To Sami Alvarado, Alexis Sattler, and Elena Craig, thank you for supporting my love of mogwai culture.
Finally, to my kids, always follow the three rules: no bright light, avoid water, and no feeding after midnight.

FROM ERIK

I want you all to know, first, that I did everything alone. Me, myself. There's no one to acknowledge except for my own—whoops, must've had a gremlin in the gears. Sorry about that. I want to thank intrepid Insight Edition editors Alexis Sattler and Sami Alvarado for bringing me on to this project and letting me have so much silly fun. To Jenn Fujikawa, thank you for letting me share some pages with you again. To Joe Dante: I appreciate you nudging *Gremlins 2* into the kind of insanity that helped shape what many guidance counselors told me was a "unique" sense of humor and thank you to the friends and employers who help me indulge in this sense of humor still. (You all know who you are; you asked me specifically not to reveal your full names.) Seriously, thank you to the many folks who have been so kind and supportive over the years, including Chelsea and Chris, Kimberly, Sara, Jason and Ashley, Heather, Evan, Tom, Erica, Ryan, and Jesse . . . to name a select few. I could mention a hundred more, but there's only so much room! You've all kept me writing, which allows me to work on fun gigs like this. Thank you.

PO Box 3088
San Rafael, CA 94912
www.insighteditions.com

Find us on Facebook: www.facebook.com/InsightEditions
Follow us on Instagram: @insighteditions

ISBN: 979-8-88663-473-0

Publisher: Raoul Goff
SVP, Group Publisher: Vanessa Lopez
VP, Creative: Chrissy Kwasnik
VP, Manufacturing: Alix Nicholaeff
Editorial Director: Paul Ruditis
Art Director: Stuart Smith
Editor: Sami Alvarado
Executive Project Editor: Maria Spano
Senior Project Editor: Mary Colgan
Production Manager: Deena Hashem
Senior Production Manager, Subsidiary Rights: Lina s Palma-Temena

Photographer: Ted Thomas
Food & Prop Stylist: Elena P Craig
Assistant Food & Prop Stylist: Patricia C Parrish
Design: Amazing15

Insight Editions, in association with Roots of Peace, will plant two trees for each tree used in the manufacturing of this book. Roots of Peace is an internationally renowned humanitarian organization dedicated to eradicating land mines worldwide and converting war-torn lands into productive farms and wildlife habitats. Roots of Peace will plant two million fruit and nut trees in Afghanistan and provide farmers there with the skills and support necessary for sustainable land use.

Manufactured in China by Insight Editions

10 9 8 7 6 5 4 3 2 1